Pro Grunt.js

James Cryer

Apress®

Pro Grunt.js

ISBN-13 (pbk): 978-1-4842-0014-8

ISBN-13 (electronic): 978-1-4842-0013-1

Managing Director: Welmoed Spahr
Lead Editor: Louise Corrigan
Technical Reviewer: Matt Gifford

Coordinating Editor: Christine Ricketts
Copy Editor: Michael Laraque
Compositor: SPi Global
Indexer: SPi Global
Artist: SPi Global

Distributed to the book trade worldwide by Springer Science+Business Media New York, 233 Spring Street, 6th Floor, New York, NY 10013. Phone 1-800-SPRINGER, fax (201) 348-4505, e-mail `orders-ny@springer-sbm.com`, or visit `www.springeronline.com`. Apress Media, LLC is a California LLC and the sole member (owner) is Springer Science + Business Media Finance Inc (SSBM Finance Inc). SSBM Finance Inc is a Delaware corporation.

For information on translations, please e-mail `rights@apress.com`, or visit `www.apress.com`.

Apress and friends of ED books may be purchased in bulk for academic, corporate, or promotional use. eBook versions and licenses are also available for most titles. For more information, reference our Special Bulk Sales–eBook Licensing web page at `www.apress.com/bulk-sales`.

Any source code or other supplementary material referenced by the author in this text is available to readers at `www.apress.com`. For detailed information about how to locate your book's source code, go to `www.apress.com/source-code/`.

Contents at a Glance

Contents

About the Author

James Cryer is a Principal Web Developer with the BBC in Cardiff, UK. At the BBC James works within the BBC Travel team, part of BBC News, as technical lead delivering the next iteration of the Travel product across multiple platforms.

Before joining the BBC, James worked with software houses within Cardiff delivering digital solutions for a variety of clients such as the Royal Navy, Investec Asset Management and UNISON. Whilst James is a front-end specialist with a passion for web performance, he has built applications in PHP, Scala, Objective C, Java, PHP, Ruby and Node. He is an active contributor to his local community, speaking at meet ups on subject matters such as cloud technologies, browser performance and developer tooling.

James enjoys technical writing, co-authoring the Yeoman project's first CodeLab and publishing tutorials in .NET magazine. Aside from his interest in technology, he also enjoys traveling with his wife and cycling.

About the Technical Reviewer

Matt Gifford is owner and primary primate at his own development consultancy company, Monkeh Works Ltd. His work primarily focuses on building mobile apps, front end development, streamlining workflows and developing full-scale web apps in a number of server-side languages.

He's a published author and presents at conferences and user groups on a variety of topics and is also a keen proponent for community resources and sharing knowledge.

He is the author of "Object-Oriented Programming in ColdFusion" and "PhoneGap Mobile Application Development Cookbook" and also contributes articles and tutorials to international industry magazines. Visit Matt at `www.monkehworks.com` or `@coldfumonkeh` on Twitter.

Acknowledgments

Firstly, I'd like to thank Ben Alman, the creator of Grunt.js. Without Ben's creation, I wouldn't have the opportunity to write this book and hopefully inspire you to re-consider your development workflow by introducing Grunt.

Next, I would like to thank everyone at Apress for working so hard to bring this book to print. In particular, I'd like to thank Louise Corrigan for working closely with me to setup the book initially and offering advice throughout the whole process. Without Christine Ricketts this book would not be published, thanks to her constant support and help to ensure I remained on track. Last but not least, I am grateful to Matt Gifford for performing the detailed technical review of the book.

Finally, without the constant support and inspiration from my wife Charlotte, this book would never have been achieved. I thank her for her endless support and understanding as I burnt the midnight oil on numerous nights to complete the book.

Introduction

Welcome to *Pro Grunt.js*. This book has been written for those who are interested in learning how Grunt.js can be use to modernize their developer workflow. Grunt can be used to automate mundane, repetitive tasks that feature in almost all mobile and web projects. Developing optimal web applications that are tuned for performance is essential to delivering a good user experience for all. We cannot make assumptions about the devices and the networks users are accessing our sites and applications from. Grunt can be used to ensure that every project we develop has a set of best practices baked in from the outset through the definition of a common set of tasks that will enable our project to be minified, linted and tested. Grunt's extensibility and large number of plugins makes it the perfect tool for quickly developing a tool belt that is re-usable across projects.

Chapter 1

This chapter introduces Grunt, providing an overview of the benefits of using a task runner like Grunt before concluding with a comparison to other popular build tools.

Chapter 2

This chapter discusses the core concepts of Grunt. Installing Grunt on a project, tasks and file matchers are also covered.

Chapter 3

This chapter is dedicated to the introduction of Grunt tasks for working with HTML and CSS. Topics such as sass compilation, html minification and CSS linting are discussed.

Chapter 4

This chapter discusses a set of Grunt tasks that can be used whilst working with JavaScript. It covers linting, minifications and documentation generation.

Chapter 5

This chapter introduces a set of Grunt plugins for working with images, SVG and icons. Image compression, SVG minification and automated sprite generation are covered.

Chapter 6

This chapter discusses setting up a local Node server to run a static website generated by Grunt locally. The topic of testing local web applications is also covered in this chapter using frameworks such as Karma.

Chapter 7

The final chapter looks at how a Grunt workflow itself can be optimized to make it more maintainable and reusable. Topics such as Grunt configuration files, optimize plugin loading, and measuring Grunt load times are discussed.

CHAPTER 1

Introducing Grunt

So, you've picked up this book with the rather unusual title, and you're probably wondering what Grunt is or, at least, what all the buzz concerning Grunt has been about for the last 24 months. To put it simply, Grunt is a JavaScript task runner. Its primary aim is to automate repetitive tasks, freeing up developers' time to concentrate on the more difficult problems they face every day.

Grunt is written in JavaScript on top of Node distributed via npm and was created by Ben Alman (`https://github.com/cowboy`). Since day one, Grunt has featured an application program interface (API) to allow developers to extend and add custom tasks to suit their own process. This high customization has lead Grunt to become extremely popular with a large ecosystem that is constantly expanding.

As a task runner, one of the core concepts of Grunt is "tasks." Each task has a set of configuration options that can be tuned to meet your specific needs. Tasks can also have multiple versions: for example, one set of configuration for development and another for production. In addition to this, Grunt offers the ability to define custom tasks. Custom tasks can combine existing tasks into a single task or add completely new functionality. In addition, Grunt has a well-documented API that enables developers to change the behavior of their task runner at runtime.

Throughout this book, Grunt will be used to demonstrate how this small yet extremely powerful tool can be used to optimize your developer workflow. Grunt is often portrayed as being a tool solely for front-end engineers; however, I will also demonstrate how projects that aren't solely front-end focused can also benefit from the introduction of Grunt.

How Can I Benefit from Grunt?

One of the key benefits and primary objectives of Grunt is automation. You may question why you need automation, when your existing workflow works for you. I hope this book will serve as encouragement and demonstrate how automation can make you more efficient.

Most developers are familiar with the tools required to perform tasks such as code linting, asset minification, and compiling CSS as part of their workflow. However, not every developer has this process automated. Some teams opt to use continuous integration as a point to build their application and perform prerelease checks. This environment is often controlled outside of the development team, with responsibilities lying elsewhere within an organization.

It is convenient to rely on your continuous integration environment to perform build tasks. As a developer, you write code, push it to your central code repository, and your continuous integration (CI) server handles the rest. However, if you have to replicate an issue locally from a production environment, this may not be the quickest process for you. With the power of Grunt, you can utilize the same build process easily within your local development and CI environment, reducing the time taken to build a production version of your application locally.

Developers working on their own or in a small team opting to use command-line or graphical user interface (GUI) tools can unify their build process through the use of Grunt. Unifying the build process will simplify the project setup and maintenance, as there will be a single process to follow.

Continuous Integration

If you are unfamiliar with CI, it is a common development practice of merging code from a team of developers into a central repository. It is often used to run unit tests, perform code analysis, and automate deployments. Most modern open source projects use TravisCI (`https://travis-ci.org/`), an open source CI environment that can be easily integrated with GitHub repositories. Other alternatives that are popular within the development community are Hudson and Jenkins, Jenkins being a fork of Hudson. Both Jenkins and Hudson have a number of plug-ins available for integrating third-party tools or systems, such as a plug-in that adds the ability to trigger builds on updates to repositories within GitHub.

Speeding Up Your Workflow

There are some fantastic tools and integrated development environments (IDEs) available to help you develop applications and sites that provide tools for common tasks, such as compiling your CSS and linting your JavaScript. However, such tools typically require an initial setup and can also lead to a disjointed workflow.

You might be wondering what is meant by a “disjointed workflow.” Consider the following scenario: You’re working a very simple one-page application with a set of JavaScript files, a CSS preprocessor, and a number of images. Before you release the application, you will have to lint your JavaScript, compile your CSS, and compress your images. For each of these problems, you can choose from a wide range of tools already in existence, such as JSHint, LESS compiler, and `pngquant`. It is likely that your IDE will lint your JavaScript and LESS compilation; however, you would have to switch to the command line to then run `pngquant`.

Switching between your browser, editor, and command-line interface while developing will distract you from focusing on the key problems that you must solve. Grunt can provide you with a solution for unifying these tasks. In addition, Grunt also automates these tasks, so that you can focus on the unique problems within your application.

Every Craftsman Needs a Toolbelt

There is no denying that the craftsmanship of front-end web development has changed dramatically over the last few years. Gone are the days when valuable development time was consumed by solving browser compatibility issues, as developers now have access to a rich set of tools that handle such trivia. Utilizing these tools enables developers to invest their time in solving more complex problems with their applications. The emergence of frameworks that solve everyday tasks, such as Bootstrap and AngularJS, have enabled developers to deliver enhanced experiences through their applications.

Increasingly, users are accessing applications from mobile devices and have an expectation that web applications should offer the same experience as native mobile applications. The increased volume of traffic to applications from mobile devices has also forced developers to rethink how they engineer their applications, adding further complexity. To combat this, a developer has to build a set of reliable tools that can be used time and time again.

Grunt should become one of your primary tools that form part of your toolbelt. Due to the modular nature of Grunt, it is quite easy to build a recipe book of tasks that can be used across multiple projects. Each task focuses on a single problem, and it is easy to mix and match configurations across projects to build a powerful set of tools for each context.

Integration with Other Tools

There is no denying that tools available for front-end engineers have dramatically improved over the last 24 months. One particular project that has seen substantial development by the community is Yeoman. Coined as a workflow instead of a framework, Yeoman consists of three key components: Yo, Grunt, and Bower. Grunt is a key player in the Yeoman project, and, as illustrated later in the book, combining Yo and Grunt together provides the ability to rapidly scaffold projects that include an automated build process.

Versioning

Another key benefit of using Grunt is that your tasks are versioned along with their configuration. As Grunt tasks within a project are installed by npm, these are easily managed using npm itself. In addition to this, the configuration changes are clearly visible to the whole team as they are versioned with the project. This builds a toolset that the whole team can learn, develop, and benefit from.

■ **Note** npm is a package manager for JavaScript, allowing developers to easily share and reuse JavaScript modules. npm handles the versioning, dependencies, and publishing of packages. Each package has metadata defined in a JSON configuration file, called `package.json`, which contains information such as name, description, version, authors, and dependencies.

Readability

Another factor contributing to Grunt's rapid growth in popularity is its readability. Grunt's task configuration is a simple JSON configuration object, making it highly readable and understandable.

Grunt also promotes the development technique of Don't Repeat Yourself (DRY), as tasks can use variables as part of their configuration. As you'll see later in the book, this also improves the readability of task configuration.

A further benefit of having a readable task runner is to dramatically reduce the time required for new team members to get up to speed on how the build process works.

Alternatives

It's good to be aware that Grunt wasn't the first task runner to automate developer workflow. There are a number of alternatives; however, Grunt stands tall among them, due to its vast ecosystem, simplicity, and speed. We'll briefly look at a few popular alternatives before delving into Grunt.

Ant

Formally known as Apache Ant, "Ant" is a Java-based build tool. Rather than specifying tasks using JavaScript, tasks are defined in an XML file in your project. Ant comes packaged with more than 100 built-in tasks, such as concatenation of files, gzipping files, and replacing contents within a file. However, these tasks are slightly more oriented toward a build process for a Java project. For example, if you want to support JavaScript linting, you will have to include a new task. To add such tasks, Ant requires the new tasks to be compiled as JAR files and referenced from the XML configuration. For those unfamiliar with Java, this might be a little daunting when you first get started. Grunt might be a better fit if your project doesn't require Java as part of the build process, as this adds an unnecessary dependency to the project.

You may consider choosing Grunt over Ant owing to the configuration format use: JSON instead of XML. Reading an Ant build file feels a little bloated, and it isn't obvious at a glance how a build process hangs together, while Grunt's JSON is leaner, and tasks can be combined into logical names.

Rake

Rake is the Ruby community's answer to Make files. Rake allows developers to define tasks using Ruby syntax. Anybody who has used the Ruby on Rails framework should be reasonably familiar with Rake, as it's used as the tool of choice for tasks such as the creation of databases, running tests, and compiling static assets.

Rake does not have a concept of task configuration. Instead, it opts for tasks that define and execute Ruby to achieve its goals. For example, there are no repositories of recipes or plug-ins available to perform common tasks. If you want to concatenate and lint your JavaScript, you will have to start from scratch and write your task before you can use it. This will obviously make it more costly to get started on your projects, as Rake doesn't offer anything up front. It is up to you to ensure that your tasks are highly configurable to increase reuse across projects.

Grunt solves the problem of having to reinvent the wheel by offering a wide selection of plug-ins. In addition, Grunt also promotes the concept of configuration over code, by providing a rich API for supporting task configuration.

Gulp

Gulp is a relatively new tool that is, like Grunt, JavaScript-based. Another similarity between Grunt and Gulp is the modular-based architecture, powered by the use of npm as a dependency manager. Gulp, like Grunt, is easy to get started; however, arguably, Gulp has more succinct task definition, as tasks are expressed in code instead of configuration.

There have been several blog posts that pit Grunt and Gulp against each other. However, there have also been counter arguments stating that both tools can coexist, owing to differences in how they achieve a common set of goals. Gulp is faster than Grunt, yet the barrier to entry is a little higher, due to its use of Node streams.

■ **Note** Grunt combines tasks in which the output of one task produces a temporary file that is picked up by the next task for processing. Gulp doesn't produce these temporary files; files are piped between each task.

Summary

In this chapter, you've received a basic overview of what Grunt is and how projects can benefit from using it. You've also explored how Grunt compares to similar alternatives available. This book should provide you with an understanding of how to set up and use Grunt on your projects, allowing you to rapidly lint, test, and optimize your applications.

CHAPTER 2

How to Use Grunt in Your Project

In the previous chapter, you received a brief introduction to Grunt and the benefits of using Grunt in your projects. This chapter will take a more detailed look at Grunt, how to install Grunt, and how to use Grunt in your projects. Before looking at Grunt itself, it is important to have a good understanding of Node.js. Grunt is built on top of Node.js, so having a good understanding of Node.js and how modules operate within Node.js will make learning and understanding Grunt easier.

Node.js

Node.js is an application platform that allows developers to implement event-driven applications built on top of Chrome's JavaScript engine, V8. As many of you will know, JavaScript originated as a client-side language; it was used to implement interactive interfaces. Node.js utilizes JavaScript as a scripting language on the server side and achieves high scalability through non-blocking I/O operations. To achieve non-blocking I/O operations, Node.js applications use asynchronous execution, whereas, traditionally, applications execute code in a given sequence. Non-blocking I/O is a process that allows other processing to continue while waiting for a response from an expensive I/O operation. For example, if a Node.js application sends a request to a remote HTTP service for data, it does not wait for a response before processing other requests. Upon the request being sent to the remote HTTP service, the Node.js application will continue to process other requests before returning to the original routine, once the remote HTTP service has responded. This ability to continue processing other requests while waiting for I/O operations can provide significant performance improvements.

Node.js was created by Ryan Dahl in 2009. His inspiration came from his experience of web sites that would continuously poll servers for updates. Dahl wanted to create a framework that was event-driven and allowed servers to push data to the browser, instead of data being polled continuously.

Node.js is available across multiple platforms: Linux, Windows, and Mac OS X. The installation process for each is relatively easy, and you will have to install Node.js before you can use Grunt.

Installing on Linux

Node.js is available to download from its source, but it is also available via most popular package managers, such as yum and aptitude. For example, on Ubuntu 12.04 and later versions, Node.js can be installed using the following:

```
sudo yum apt-get install Node.js
```

For more specific details on installing Node.js on your distribution of Linux, refer to the official documentation (`https://github.com/joyent/node/wiki/Installing-Node.js-via-package-manager`).

Installing on Windows

For readers using Windows, head over to `http://nodejs.org/` and download the Windows installer. Once you have completed the installation process, Node.js will be available.

Installing on Mac OS X

On Mac OS X, there is an official installer available from `http://nodejs.org`; however, you may wish to install the latest version from your package manager of choice. Node.js is available for the most popular package managers on the Mac OS X platform.

To install Node.js with Homebrew, use the following:

```
brew install node
```

Alternatively, to install Node.js with MacPorts, use the following:

```
sudo port install Node.js
```

Confirming Your Installation

After completing the preceding installation steps, Node.js will be available to you. As part of the installation npm, a package manager, for now, was also installed. Prior to version 0.6.3 of Node.js, npm was installed separately. To confirm that node and npm are available, open the terminal, or command prompt in Windows, and type the following:

```
node --version
npm -version
```

You should have a similar version number to the one shown in Figure 2-1 in the respective environments.

For the remainder the book, we will be using Node.js version 0.10.26 and npm version 1.4.3, as illustrated in Figure 2-1.

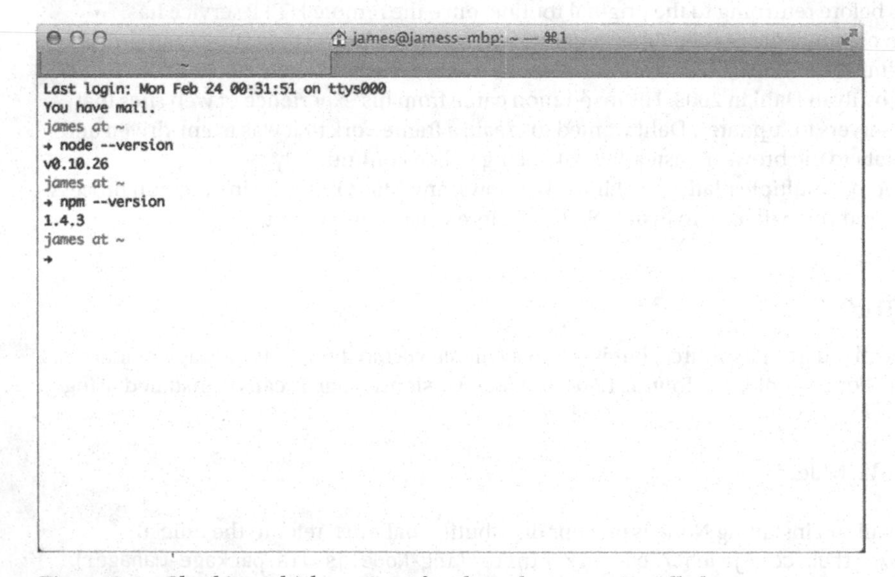

***Figure 2-1.** Checking which version of node and npm are installed*

npm

npm provides a convenient way to create, share, and install Node.js packages across several projects. Packages are published to a central npm registry allowing developers from across the globe to install and reuse these packages within their own project. npm provides a standard approach to defining JavaScript packages that can be easily reused across projects. Each package has a name, description, author(s), and a set of dependencies.

As mentioned in the previous chapter, Grunt uses a plug-in-based architecture, allowing developers to mix and match tasks across projects. To achieve this extreme flexibility, Grunt harnesses the existing modularization offered by Node.js and npm. Each Grunt plug-in is a Node.js package that can be installed using npm.

npm allows developers to define a package's dependencies. When others install a package, npm manages the installation and its dependencies so that you don't have to worry.

Before taking a first look at Grunt, I'll cover two key features of Node.js and npm that we will use when installing and using Grunt.

Finding Modules

npm allows developers to search a registry of all Node.js packages. Searches against a registry accept one or more search terms. A search term can also be a regular expression, these start with a /.

To search for a package, open the command line or command prompt and enter

```
npm search grunt
```

This will return all the Node.js packages that contain the word *grunt* in the title, description, author, and/or tags. You will see later in the chapter how to define this metadata for a package. The results of your search should look similar to those shown in Figure 2-2, with the search term highlighted.

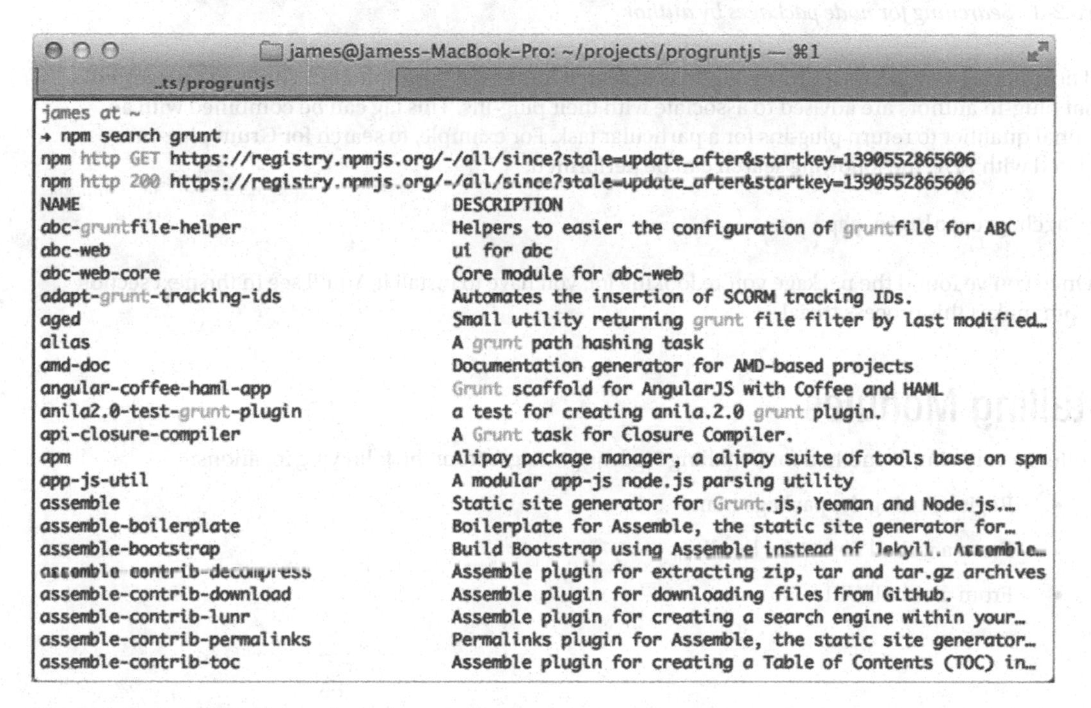

Figure 2-2. *Searching for node packages with npm*

The first time npm search is run against a repository, a local index is built. This local index contains a reference to all the packages within the searched repository. The local index is intended to speed up future searches but may take some time if you run the search command while on a small network.

The results returned from a search contain the module name and the description in columns, respectively. If a search is performed for a particular package author, the author column is also displayed. For example, a search for "jrcryer"

```
npm search jrcryer
```

will return all plug-ins written by me (see Figure 2-3).

```
james@Jamess-MacBook-Pro: ~/projects/progruntjs — ⌘1
..ts/progruntjs
james at ~/projects/progruntjs                                          ±(master)
→ npm search jrcryer
NAME                      DESCRIPTION                                          AUTHOR   DATE
generator-finatra         Yeoman generator for Finatra framework               =jrcryer 2014-
generator-mean            A Yeoman generator for MEAN stack, inspired by mean.io =jrcryer 2014-
generator-pattern-primer  Yeoman generator for pattern priming                 =jrcryer 2014-
grunt-har-gen             Grunt plugin for generating HAR files from a series of URLs =jrcryer 2013-
grunt-pagespeed           Grunt plugin for running Google PageSpeed Insights.  =jrcryer 2014-
grunt-phpspec             Grunt plugin for running PHPSpecs.                   =jrcryer 2013-
grunt-rcukes              Grunt plugin for running ruby cucumber.              =jrcryer 2013-
phpunit-watchr            A simple script to watch a directories and run phpunit tests =jrcryer 2012-
npm http GET https://registry.npmjs.org/-/all/since?stale=update_after&startkey=1393291396159
james at ~/projects/progruntjs                                          ±(master)
→ _
```

Figure 2-3. Searching for node packages by author

The quickest way to find a Grunt plug-in is to search for the tag "gruntplugin." This is the suggested tag that plug-in authors are advised to associate with their plug-ins. This tag can be combined with an additional qualifier to return plug-ins for a particular task. For example, to search for Grunt plug-ins associated with PHP, the following search can be performed:

```
npm search gruntplugin php
```

Once you've found the package you're looking for, you have to install it. You'll see in the next section how npm makes this process trivial.

Installing Modules

npm offers a very simple method for installing Node.js packages from the following locations:

- Registry using the package name
- From a tarball file stored locally
- From a tarball URL

- From a folder
- For example, to install request, the popular Node.js HTTP client, use the following command:

```
npm install request
```

This will begin to install the request package into a folder, `node_modules`, inside the current directory. Inside the `node_modules` folder, npm will also install the dependencies that request requires. As part of the installation process, npm will list all the packages it is attempting to install. As request installs, your command-line interface should look similar to the output in Figure 2-4.

```
james@Jamess-MacBook-Pro: ~/projects/progruntjs — ⌘1
..ts/progruntjs
npm http 200 https://registry.npmjs.org/ctype/0.5.2
npm http GET https://registry.npmjs.org/ctype/-/ctype-0.5.2.tgz
npm http 304 https://registry.npmjs.org/async
npm http GET https://registry.npmjs.org/delayed-stream/0.0.5
npm http 304 https://registry.npmjs.org/boom
npm http 304 https://registry.npmjs.org/cryptiles
npm http 200 https://registry.npmjs.org/punycode
npm http GET https://registry.npmjs.org/punycode/-/punycode-1.2.4.tgz
npm http 304 https://registry.npmjs.org/sntp
npm http 304 https://registry.npmjs.org/delayed-stream/0.0.5
npm http 200 https://registry.npmjs.org/hoek
npm http 200 https://registry.npmjs.org/ctype/-/ctype-0.5.2.tgz
npm http 200 https://registry.npmjs.org/punycode/-/punycode-1.2.4.tgz
request@2.34.0 node_modules/request
├── json-stringify-safe@5.0.0
├── forever-agent@0.5.2
├── aws-sign2@0.5.0
├── qs@0.6.6
├── tunnel-agent@0.3.0
├── oauth-sign@0.3.0
├── mime@1.2.11
├── node-uuid@1.4.1
├── form-data@0.1.2 (async@0.2.10, combined-stream@0.0.4)
├── hawk@1.0.0 (cryptiles@0.2.2, sntp@0.2.4, boom@0.4.2, hoek@0.9.1)
├── tough-cookie@0.12.1 (punycode@1.2.4)
```

Figure 2-4. *Using npm to install the package called request*

Modules

As seen in the preceding figure, it is relatively easy to discover and install new packages with npm. Before starting our exploration into the use of Grunt, it is important to understand what a Node.js module consists of.

The Node.js module system is an implementation the CommonJS module system. The CommonJS specification was devised to address how JavaScript modules should be written to improve interoperability. It aims to bridge the gap that JavaScript does not currently solve, by allowing developers to create clearly defined modules that can be shared across projects.

In the simplest of forms, a module is a JavaScript file. Node.js provides the ability for developers to include the JavaScript defined in one file into another and use its functionality. The simplest module is as follows:

```
exports.test = "value";
```

The preceding can be saved in a file titled `something.js` and defines a single property for the module `test`. This could then be reused as follows:

```
var mod = require('./something');
console.log(mod.test);
```

In the preceding code sample, we're including the module `something` and referencing the module as `mod` locally. We can then use the property `test` within our application by referencing it on `mod`. The preceding application will output the string `value` to the command line.

As you can see, inside the module there is a JavaScript object called `exports`. As Node.js includes a module, it creates a new context and injects the `exports` object. The `exports` object is then returned as part of a call to `require`. To expose any functionality publically as part of a Node.js module, properties can be assigned to the `exports` object. Let's take a look at another example (Listing 2-1) with a module that exposes a function.

Listing 2-1. Exporting a Function As Part of a Node.js Module

```
exports.add = function(a, b) {
  return a + b;
};
```

The preceding module, when saved as `something.js`, can then be used as follows (Listing 2-2):

Listing 2-2. Calling a Function from an Imported Module

```
var simple = require('./something');
console.log(simple.add(1,2));
```

Running this application will output "3" to the command line.

The use of modules also provides the ability to hide the implementation of complex functionality within a module while exposing a simplified interface for users of the module. Following (Listing 2-3) is a module that hides the property `display` from users of the module.

Listing 2-3. Node.js Module Demonstrating Private Variables

```
var display = false;

exports = {
  isHidden: function() {
     return display === false;
  },
  hide: function() {
     display = false;
  },
  show: function() {
     display = true;
  }
};
```

In the preceding example, the module allows a user of this module to manipulate the display property through the `hide` and `show` methods.

At this stage, you might be wondering how this relates to Grunt. As mentioned earlier, Grunt plug-ins are Node.js packages. Grunt plug-ins typically consist of one or more modules and often rely on other Node.js packages to achieve their goal. Having a good understanding of Node.js, its module system, and how it operates will put you in great stead when using Grunt on your projects. Thus far, you've seen how to load modules relative to the current module. These are known as File Modules. In addition to File Modules, modules can be loaded from the `node_modules` directory. `node_modules` is the directory with which npm will create and install your project dependencies when you run the npm install command. Let's take a quick look at an example of this.

Loading Modules from node_modules

In our example, we will once again install the Node.js package called request, using the following:

```
npm install request
```

Once npm has completed the install, you will notice that a new folder has been created in your current folder (see Figure 2-5). If you open the `node_modules` folder, you will see another folder matching the name of the Node.js package that has been installed. The `request` folder contains the contents of the request package.

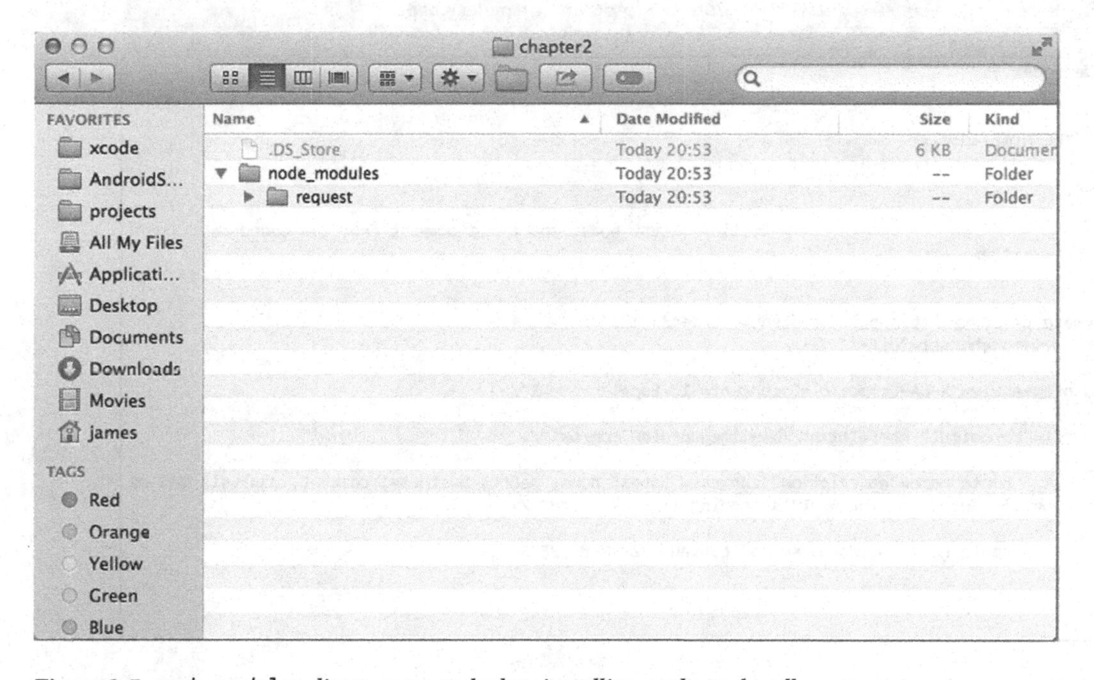

Figure 2-5. *`node_modules` directory created when installing packages locally*

Now that the package is installed, it is now available for use in our project. Following (Listing 2-4) is a sample application that loads the request module and uses it to make a request for `'http://www.guardian.co.uk'`.

Listing 2-4. Loading and Using the request Module

```
var request = require('request');

request.get('http://www.guardian.co.uk', function(error, response, body) {
  if (!error && response.statusCode == 200) {
    console.log(body);
  }
});
```

The preceding sample application can be saved to `index.js` alongside the `node_modules` directory. It can then be run from the command line, as follows:

```
node index.js
```

The preceding will output the HTML contents of the *Guardian* home page (see Figure 2-6). On the first line of the application, we include the request package and store a reference to it with the variable named `request`. This allows us to use functions defined within the package within our own application. In our example, we use the get method that the request package offers, which allows us to send an HTTP `GET` request to the supplied URL.

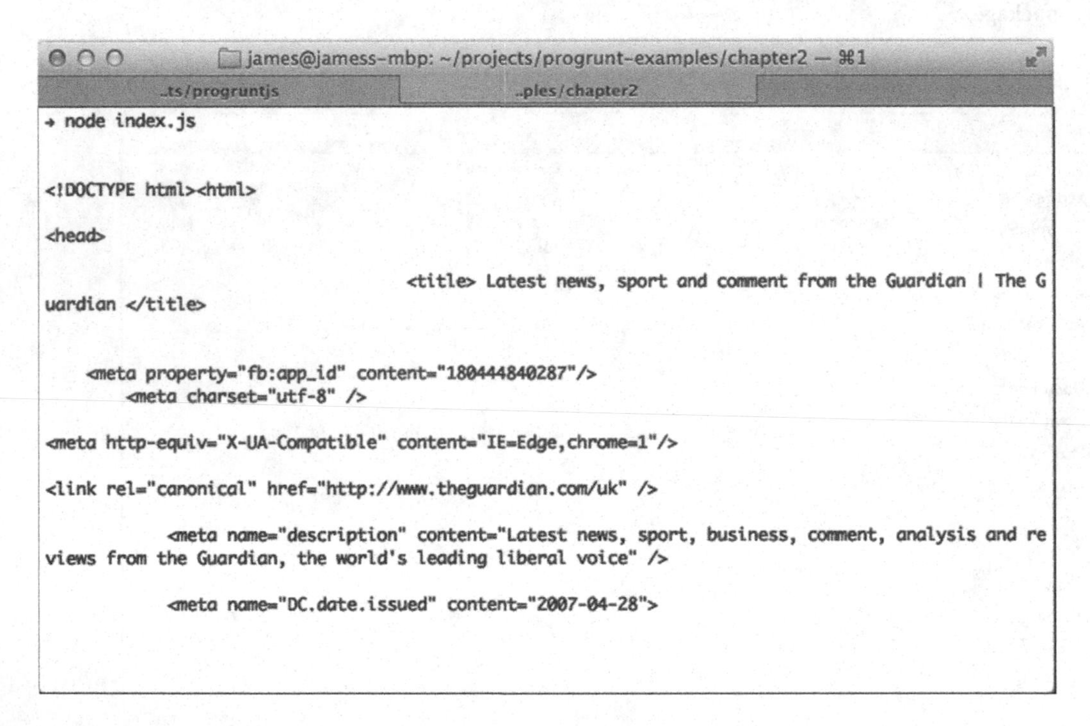

Figure 2-6. *Sample application output HTML from Guardian web site*

The important thing to note here is the lack of `/`, `../`," or `./` at the start of `require`. If the module identifier passed to `require` is not a core Node.js module and does not start with `/`, `../`, or `./`, Node.js will attempt to load the module from the current module's parent directory, appended with "`node_modules`." If the module is not found, it moves to the parent directory, and so on.

For example, if our application is located at `/Users/james/projects/progrunt/index.js`, Node.js will attempt to load the `request` package at the following locations:

- `/Users/james/projects/progrunt/node_modules/request`
- `/Users/james/projects/node_modules/request`
- `/Users/james/node_modules/request`
- `/Users/node_modules/request`
- `/node_modules/request`

This allows applications to localize their dependencies, so that they do not clash (see Figure 2-7).

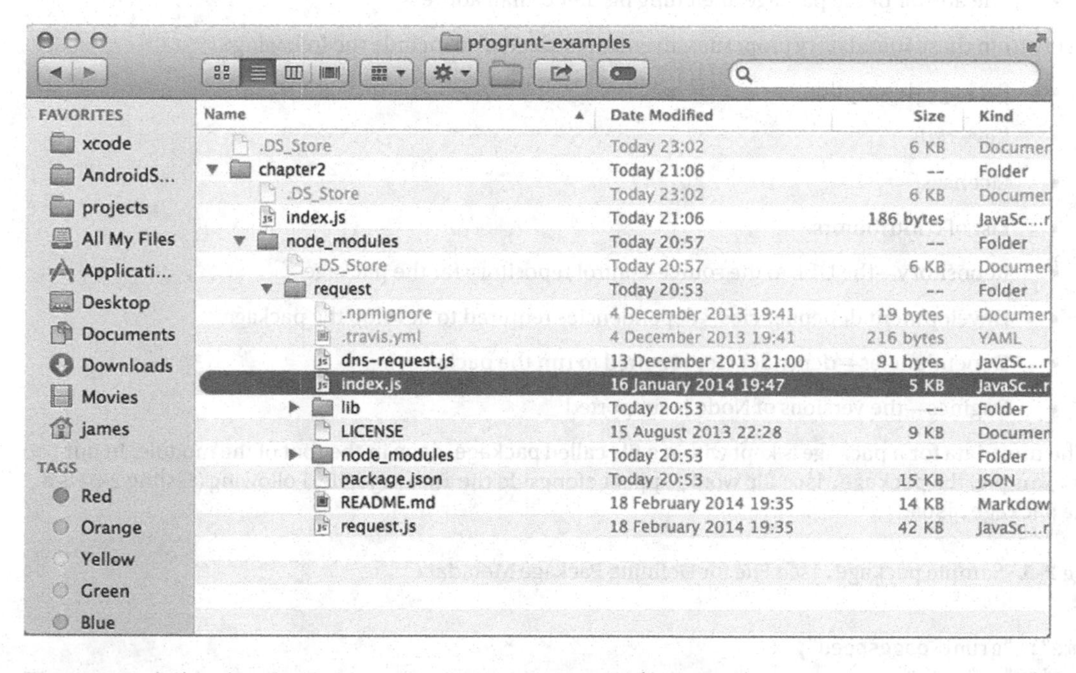

Figure 2-7. *`index.js` is loaded from `request` when `require('request');` is run*

The sharp-eyed among you might have noticed that in our earlier examples, we were loading files, but `request` is being loaded from a directory. Node.js also supports loading modules from folders. Node.js will attempt to load a module from a folder, using the following rules:

- From the main property from the `package.json` inside the folder
- `index.js` file
- `index.node` file

In our example, the request package contains matches on the first rule and second rule.

This concludes the various approaches Node.js takes to load packages. It has been important to visit each approach, as you will use these throughout the remainder of the book. Next, we will look at how to define properties and dependencies for your Node.js projects. Again, this is an important section to understand, as you'll use the same techniques when using Grunt on a project.

Defining Node.js Projects

Node.js provides a convenient method for defining metadata for a package. This metadata is used when searching for a package via npm. It is also used on the npm site, `www.npmjs.org`, to display useful information to allow developers to understand what a package does and how it can be used. In addition, the metadata also allows developers to define the dependencies needed to develop the package and the dependencies needed to run the package.

Package metadata must include the following:

- A package name
- The current version of the package
- The author of the package, including his/her e-mail address

Aside from these mandatory properties, the metadata can also include the following:

- Package description
- Keywords
- Licenses
- List of contributors
- Repository—the URL to the source-control repository for the package
- Development dependencies—dependencies required to develop the package
- Dependencies—dependencies required to run the package
- Engines—the versions of Node.js supported

The metadata for a package is kept within a file called `package.json` in the root of the module. In our earlier example, the `package.json` file would appear alongside the `index.js` file. Following (Listing 2-5) is a sample `package.json`:

Listing 2-5. Sample `package.json` File for Defining Package Metadata

```
{
  "name": "grunt-pagespeed",
  "version": "0.1.2",
  "description": "Grunt plugin for running Google PageSpeed Insights.",
  "homepage": "https://github.com/jrcryer/grunt-pagespeed",
  "author": {
    "name": "James Cryer",
    "email": "chat@jamescryer.com",
    "url": "http://www.jamescryer.com/"
  },
  "repository": {
    "type": "git",
    "url": "git://github.com/jrcryer/grunt-pagespeed.git"
  },
  "contributors": [],
  "main": "Gruntfile.coffee",
  "engines": {
    "node": ">=0.8.0"
```

```
  },
  "devDependencies": {
    "grunt": "~0.4.1"
  },
  "dependencies": {
    "googleapis": "~0.6.1"
  },
  "keywords": [
    "gruntplugin",
    "pagespeed",
    "insights",
    "grunt",
    "performance"
  ]
}
```

The preceding is a copy of the `package.json` from my Grunt plug-in for running pagespeed insights against sites. The important properties to note in the preceding example are `devDependencies` and `dependencies`. These are the properties that allow us to define other Node.js packages required for our project. Later in this chapter, you will see how Grunt plug-in dependencies appear here.

npm bundles a handy command for bootstrapping your projects. It asks a set of questions and generates a `package.json` file based on your answers. Let's revisit our earlier example and generate a `package.json` for the project. First, ensure that you are in the root folder of the project (the folder containing `index.js`) and run the following:

```
npm init
```

npm will then prompt you to answer a series of questions (see Figure 2-8).

```
npm init — ⌘1
..ts/progruntjs | npm
Press ^C at any time to quit.
name: (chapter2) guardian-grabber
version: (0.0.0) 0.0.1
description:
entry point: (index.js)
test command:
git repository:
keywords:
author: James Cryer
license: (ISC)
About to write to /Users/james/projects/progrunt-examples/chapter2/package.json:

{
  "name": "guardian-grabber",
  "version": "0.0.1",
  "description": "",
  "main": "index.js",
  "dependencies": {
    "request": "~2.34.0"
  },
  "devDependencies": {},
  "scripts": {
    "test": "echo \"Error: no test specified\" && exit 1"
  },
  "author": "James Cryer",
```

Figure 2-8. *Sample application output HTML from Guardian web site*

npm will present you with the `package.json` that is about to be generated and ask whether it is correct. If you select yes, you will notice that you now have a `package.json` file in the root of the project. You may have also noticed that npm is clever enough to detect that we've already installed `request` and added it to the generated `package.json` file.

Once the `package.json` file is added your project, you have to add an additional flag when installing packages, to ensure that npm updates the `package.json`. For example, if we want to add a popular unit-testing framework `nodeunit` to our project, we would have to run the following:

```
npm install nodeunit -save
```

The `-save` flag informs npm that we wish to add this package as a dependency. Alternatively, we could have used `--save-dev` to add the package to the development dependencies. After running the preceding command, the `package.json` file should now look similar to Listing 2-6.

Listing 2-6. `package.json` after Installing `nodeunit`

```
{
  "name": "guardian-grabber",
  "version": "0.0.1",
  "description": "",
  "main": "index.js",
  "dependencies": {
    "request": "~2.34.0",
    "nodeunit": "^0.8.6"
  },
  "devDependencies": {},
  "scripts": {
    "test": "echo \"Error: no test specified\" && exit 1"
  },
  "author": "James Cryer",
  "license": "ISC"
}
```

Now that I've established what a Node.js package is and how we can search and install them within our own projects, we can move on to Grunt itself.

Grunt

As mentioned previously, Grunt plug-ins are Node.js packages. However, I failed to mention that Grunt is itself a Node.js package as well. Throughout this book, we will be using Grunt version 0.4.x. It is important to note the version of Grunt, as there were some significant changes between version 0.3.x and 0.4.x. The biggest change was to split the Grunt package into three separate packages:

- `grunt-cli`
- `grunt`
- `grunt-init`

The reasons behind this design decision will be made clear shortly. First, let's install the first package, `grunt-cli`, by running the following:

```
npm install -g grunt-cli
```

This will install the Grunt command-line interface globally. This will make the `grunt` command available in your command line (for OS X, *nix, or BSD, etc.), or command prompt on Windows. Depending on your setup, the preceding command may have to be run using sudo or as administrator on the respective platforms.

Once `grunt-cli` has been installed, you should be able to run the following:

```
grunt -version
```

And you should see a similar output to the one in Figure 2-9.

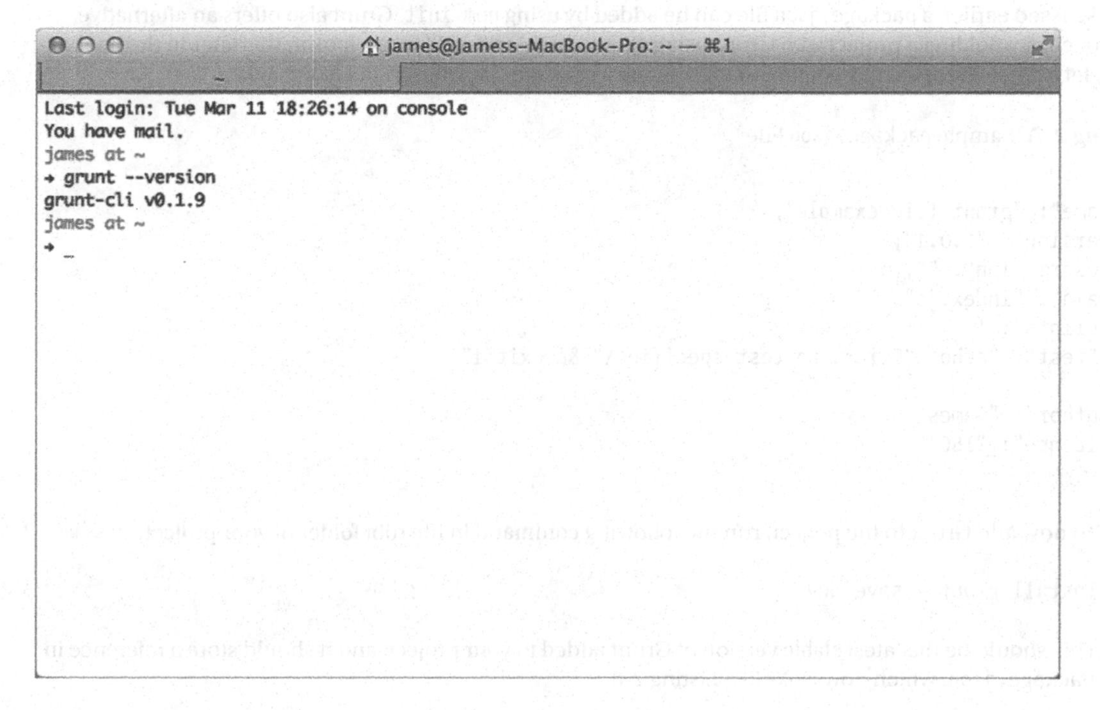

Figure 2-9. *Grunt version output on command line*

The Grunt command-line interface is not a task runner itself; it is responsible for running the local version of Grunt install on each project. This reduces the need to install the task runner globally and allows projects to have different versions of Grunt installed, if needed.

The next step to using Grunt on a project is to install the second Grunt package, called `grunt`.

Creating a New Project to Work with Grunt

To use Grunt in a project, two specific files are required:

- package.json
- Gruntfile

We've already seen package.json files, as part of our exploration into Node.js modules. This file will contain a development dependency on grunt itself and the associated plug-ins required for the project.

The Gruntfile, either Gruntfile.js or Gruntfile.coffee, is the file that contains the configuration of your tasks and/or definition of custom tasks.

Adding Grunt and Plug-ins to Your Project

As discussed earlier, a package.json file can be added by using npm init. Grunt also offers an alternative approach, scaffolding a project with Grunt using grunt-init, and we'll take a look at this later in the book. First, let's reuse the npm init command to generate a package.json file, as in Listing 2-7.

Listing 2-7. Sample package.json File

```
{
  "name": "grunt-file-example",
  "version": "0.0.1",
  "description": "",
  "main": "index.js",
  "scripts": {
    "test": "echo \"Error: no test specified\" && exit 1"
  },
  "author": "James",
  "license": "ISC"
}
```

To now add Grunt to the project, run the following command in the root folder of your project:

```
npm install grunt --save-dev
```

This should be the latest stable version of Grunt added to your project, and it should store a reference in your package.json, which now looks like Listing 2-8.

Listing 2-8. Updated package.json with Grunt Dependency Added

```
{
  "name": "grunt-file-example",
  "version": "0.0.1",
  "description": "",
  "main": "index.js",
  "scripts": {
    "test": "echo \"Error: no test specified\" && exit 1"
  },
```

```
  "author": "James",
  "license": "ISC",
  "devDependencies": {
    "grunt": "^0.4.3"
  }
}
```

Note: devDependencies has been added to the end of the file, and grunt has been referenced. If you rerun the grunt command as follows, the output displays the version of grunt-cli and Grunt packages (see Figure 2-10):

```
grunt -version
```

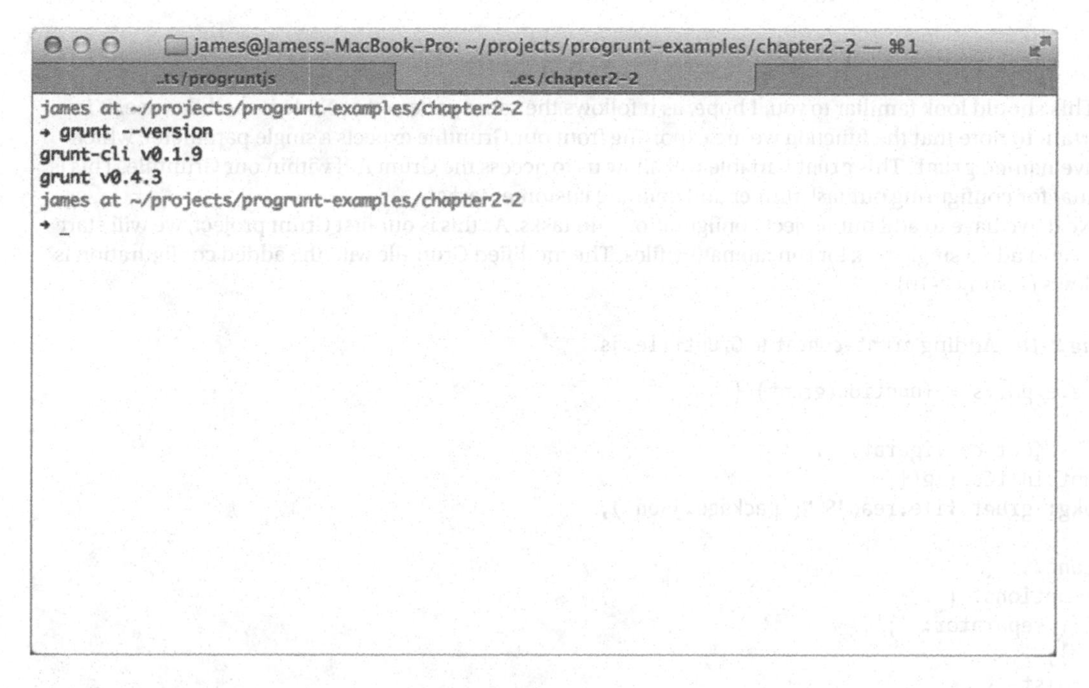

Figure 2-10. *Grunt version output on command line*

At this stage, if you run the grunt command from within your project without any other flags, you will see an error. This error informs you that it is unable to find a Gruntfile.

Create a new file in the root of your project and call it Gruntfile.js. This will create a JavaScript Gruntfile; however, if you would like to use CoffeeScript instead, save the file as Gruntfile.coffee. Throughout the book, all Gruntfiles will use JavaScript; however, I would recommend that you try writing your Gruntfiles using CoffeeScript. I personally favor CoffeeScript over JavaScript for this particular task, as it offers a cleaner and more readable configuration file.

A Gruntfile consists of the following:

- The module exports, sometimes referred to the "wrapper" function
- Project and task configuration
- Loading Grunt plug-ins and tasks
- Custom tasks

Let's add the preceding to our `Gruntfile.js` file. First, we have to add the module's exports statement to the Gruntfile (see Listing 2-9).

Listing 2-9. Start of a `Gruntfile.js`

```
module.exports = function(grunt) {

};
```

This should look familiar to you, I hope, as it follows the same pattern that Node.js modules use. It is important to note that the function we are exporting from our Gruntfile expects a single parameter, which we have named `grunt`. This `grunt` variable will allow us to access the Grunt API within our Gruntfile. This is essential for configuring our task runner and defining customer tasks.

Next, we have to add our project configuration and tasks. As this is our first Grunt project, we will start simply and add a single task for concatenating files. The modified Gruntfile with the added configuration is as follows (Listing 2-10):

Listing 2-10. Adding `grunt-concat` to `Gruntfile.js`

```
module.exports = function(grunt) {

  // Project configuration.
  grunt.initConfig({
    pkg: grunt.file.readJSON('package.json'),

    concat: {
      options: {
        separator: ';',
      },
      dist: {
        src: ['src/fileA.js', 'src/fileB.js'],
        dest: 'dist/built.js',
      }
    }
});
};
```

As you can see, there has been quite a number of lines added to the file. The first new line is a call to `grunt.initConfig`. This function initializes the configuration for the current project and expects a configuration object to be passed to it. A configuration object is a fancy name for a simple JavaScript object. Nearly every Gruntfile you write will contain a call to this function.

Next, let's inspect the configuration object passed to the initConfig call. There are two top-level properties: pkg and concat. The first property, pkg, stores a reference to contents of package.json for the project. It can be useful sometimes to use properties from our project definition within our Gruntfile. We will explore how to use these properties later in the book. The second property, concat, is our first task configuration.

The Grunt plug-in we will use in this first project is grunt-contrib-concat. This plug-in has a task defined as concat, hence we can define our configuration for this task by using the same key. The next two key properties defined within concat are options and dist. options allows us, as developers, to override the defaults provided by the plug-in author. In our example, we're overriding the default value for the separator option by specifying the character ;. The dist property is known as a *target*. Targets allow us to configure a given task in multiple contexts and provide alternative options for each. In our first example, our target is used to define the input and output files for our task. The task will search for two files, fileA.js and fileB.js, in a folder src/. These will be merged, and the output will be stored in dist/built.js.

At the moment, our Gruntfile is not valid, as we've not loaded our plug-in. Loading plug-ins is trivial, as Grunt provides an easy-to-use API to load each task. Update our Gruntfile by adding the following (Listing 2-11):

Listing 2-11. Add loadNpmTasks to the File, to Load a Plug-in

```
module.exports = function(grunt) {

  // Project configuration.
  grunt.initConfig({
    pkg: grunt.file.readJSON('package.json'),

    concat: {
      options: {
        separator: ';',
      },
      dist: {
        src: ['src/fileA.js', 'src/fileB.js'],
        dest: 'dist/built.js',
      }
    }
  });

  // Load the plugin that provides the "concat" task.
  grunt.loadNpmTasks('grunt-contrib-concat');
};
```

The additional line adds a call to the loadNpmTasks function. This function is responsible for loading tasks from a specific plug-in and expects the plug-in's name to be passed to it.

Before we can try to run our Gruntfile, we have one final statement to add to Gruntfile. Add the following line (Listing 2-12) directly after the call to loadNpmTasks.

Listing 2-12. Defining a Default Task to Be Run When Grunt Is Run Without a Task Name

```
// Default task(s).
grunt.registerTask('default', ['concat']);
```

This final line defines a default task that will be run each time someone runs the `grunt` command from within our project without passing any other values. If the plug-in is missing from our `node_modules` folder, Grunt will fail to run, as shown in Figure 2-11.

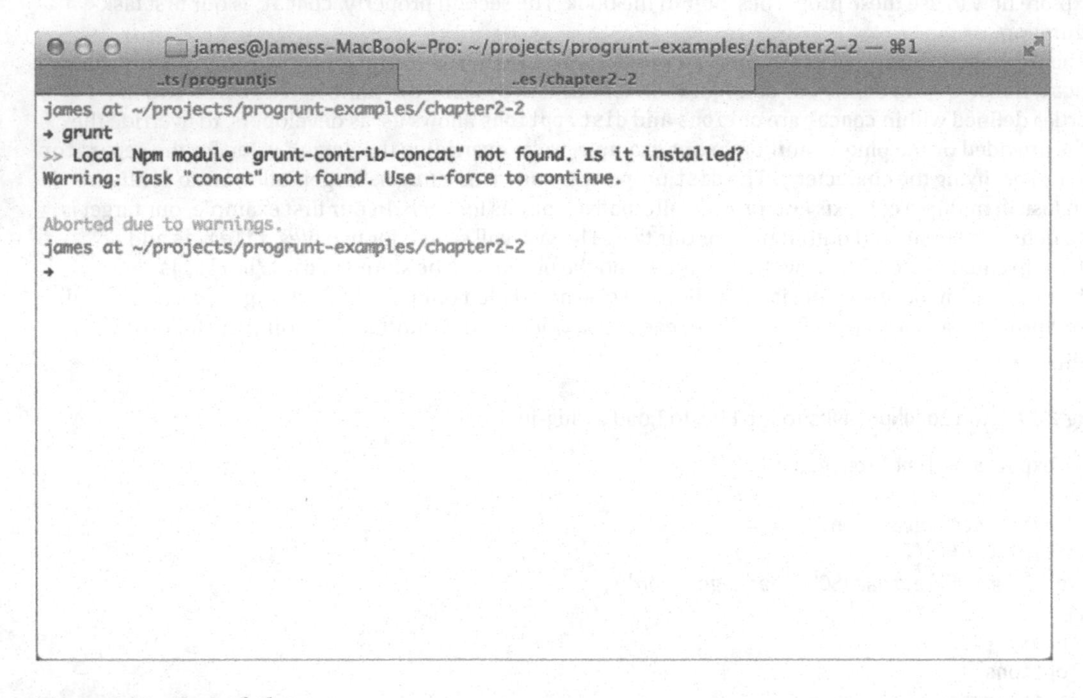

Figure 2-11. *Grunt fails to run*

At this point, we have our first complete Gruntfile. Save the file and return to your command line. While inside the root folder, running `grunt` will return an error, as we've not installed the grunt-contrib-concat plug-in yet. To add this plug-in to our project, run the following:

```
npm install grunt-contrib-concat --save-dev
```

Note that our plug-in is a Node.js package, and we're also storing a dependency inside our `package.json` (by passing `--save-dev` to the `install` command). Rerunning the `grunt` command will now yield a success message. However, our output file, `built.js`, in the `dist` folder is currently empty, as our source files do not exist.

Add a new folder called `src` to the project. Inside this file, create `fileA.js` and `fileB.js`. Inside each of the files, put two different pieces of content. (I'd suggest "A" and "B," respectively). Rerunning the grunt task, the `built.js` file should now contain the contents of `fileA.js` and `fileB.js` combined and separated by a ; (see Figure 2-12).

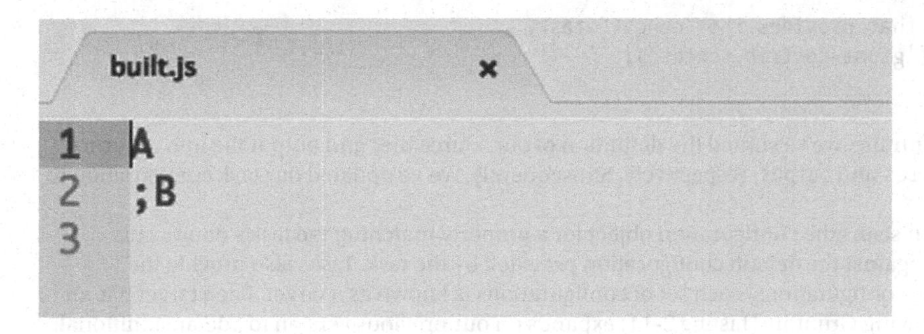

***Figure 2-12.** Output from concentation*

So we've successfully installed, set up, and run Grunt on the project. Before exploring the various ways Grunt can optimize our workflow, it is important to cover the key concepts behind Grunt. Let's start with configuring our tasks.

Configuring Tasks

As explained previously, the configuration for tasks is contained within a Gruntfile for a project. Inside this Gruntfile, configuration is passed to Grunt via the `grunt.initConfig` method. The majority of the configuration passed to `grunt.initConfig` will be under a task named properties, but it may also contain arbitrary data. If the properties in the configuration clash with task names, they will be ignored.

As the Gruntfile is JavaScript, or CoffeeScript, if you choose, the configuration is not limited strictly to JSON. This makes the task configuration extremely powerful, as it can be programmatically generated. To illustrate this principle, let's revisit our first Gruntfile and specify our files location as part of the configuration (see Listing 2-13).

Listing 2-13. Using Variables in Our Gruntfile

```
module.exports = function(grunt) {

  var app_files = ['src/fileA.js', 'src/fileB.js'],
         output = 'dist/built.js';

  // Project configuration.
  grunt.initConfig({
    pkg: grunt.file.readJSON('package.json'),

    concat: {
      options: {
        separator: ';',
      },
      dist: {
        src: app_files,
        dest: output
      }
    }
  });
```

```
  // Load the plugin that provides the "concat" task.
  grunt.loadNpmTasks('grunt-contrib-concat');
};
```

In the preceding Gruntfile, we've shifted the definition of our source files and output file into arbitrary properties called `app_files` and `output`, respectively. Subsequently, we've updated our task configuration to use these properties.

When grunt is run, it scans the configuration object for a property matching the task's name. This configuration is applied against the default configuration provided by the task. Tasks also provide the ability to specify multiple configurations; each set of configurations is known as a target. Each target has an arbitrary name. The following Gruntfile (Listing 2-14) expands on our previous version to add an additional target called test.

Listing 2-14. Multiple Targets Allow Us to Configure a Task from the Same Gruntfile in Multiple Ways

```
module.exports = function(grunt) {

  var app_files = ['src/fileA.js', 'src/fileB.js'],
         output = 'dist/built.js',
    test_output = 'test/built.js';

  // Project configuration.
  grunt.initConfig({
    pkg: grunt.file.readJSON('package.json'),

    concat: {
      options: {
        separator: ';',
      },
      dist: {
        src: app_files,
        dest: output
      },
      test: {
        src: app_files,
        dest: test_output
      }
    }
  });

  // Load the plugin that provides the "concat" task.
  grunt.loadNpmTasks('grunt-contrib-concat');
};
```

With the additional target, we output our concatentated file to a new location, the `test` folder. Grunt provides the ability to run a specific target or all targets. To run a specific target, the following command can be used:

```
grunt concat:test
```

The preceding command will run the task named `concat` and the target with the name `test` only. To run all targets, for a given task, the target can be omitted, as demonstrated in the following code. Running the command will run both the `dist` and `test` target sequentially.

```
grunt concat
```

This will iterate through each target and execute them in turn. The output of the preceding command can be seen in Figure 2-13.

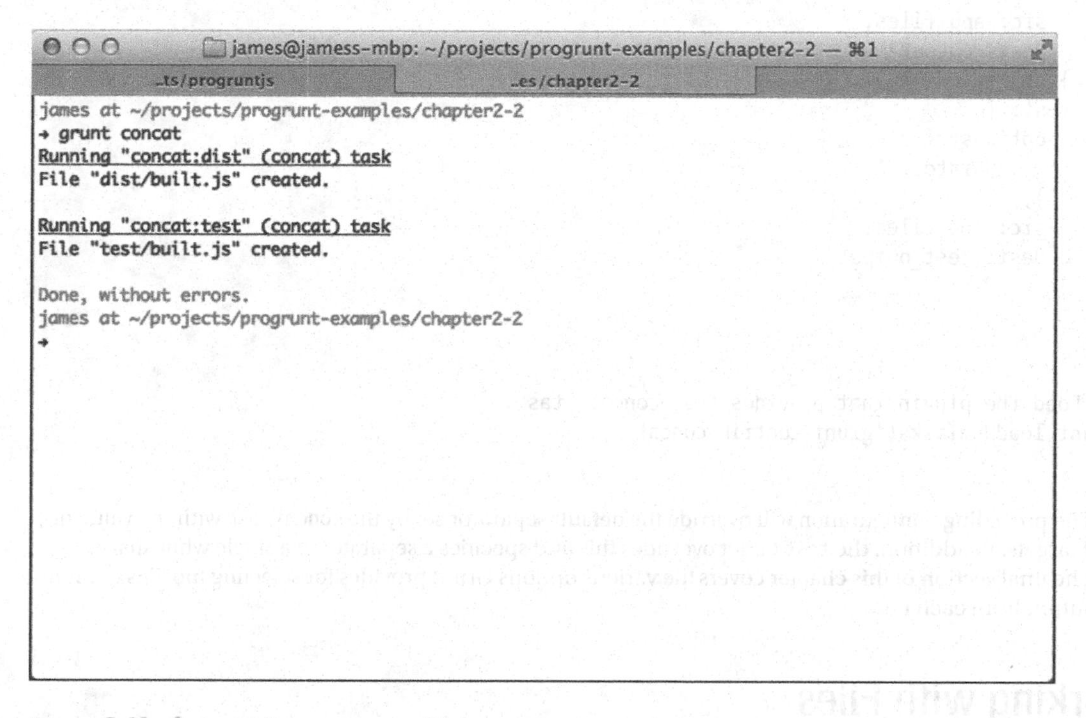

Figure 2-13. *Output when running multiple targets*

Within a task configuration, an `options` parameter can be specified to override the defaults set by a task. These options can be overridden by target-level options. Target-level options are defined by an `options` property within a target. In the following example (Listing 2-15), our Gruntfile has been modified to change the separator for the `test` target.

Listing 2-15. An Example of Using Options

```
module.exports = function(grunt) {

  var app_files = ['src/fileA.js', 'src/fileB.js'],
      output = 'dist/built.js',
    test_output = 'test/built.js';
```

```
  // Project configuration.
  grunt.initConfig({
    pkg: grunt.file.readJSON('package.json'),

    concat: {
      options: {
        separator: ';',
      },
      dist: {
        src: app_files,
        dest: output
      },
      test: {
        options: {
          separator: ' ',
        },
        src: app_files,
        dest: test_output
      }
    }
  });

  // Load the plugin that provides the "concat" task.
  grunt.loadNpmTasks('grunt-contrib-concat');
};
```

The preceding configuration will override the default separator set by the `concat` task with the value of ; for all targets. In addition, the `test` target overrides this and specifies a separator of a single whitespace.

The final section of this chapter covers the various options Grunt provides for selecting the files to input and output from each task.

Working with Files

Grunt provides a rich and powerful API for selecting the files that a task will operate on. There are a variety of methods for declaring the source and destination file mappings for each task, each varying in terms of complexity and flexibility.

Compact Format

The compact file format is commonly used for read-only tasks. As it accepts a single source-destination file mapping, the src property does not require a matching `dest` property. It would be used for tasks that operate on a set of files and report back the status for these files. An example of such a task might be a unit test runner that operates on a set of test cases and reports the outcome of each test.

Following is an example of the compact file format (Listing 2-16) using the grunt-mocha-test plug-in. For those unfamiliar with Mocha (`http://mochajs.org/`), it is a JavaScript test runner.

Listing 2-16. Using the Compact File Format to Run Mocha Tests

```
module.exports = function(grunt) {

  grunt.initConfig({
    // Configure a mochaTest task
    mochaTest: {
      test: {
        options: {
          reporter: 'spec'
        },
        src: ['test/**/*.js']
      }
    }
  });

  // Add the grunt-mocha-test tasks.
  grunt.loadNpmTasks('grunt-mocha-test');
  grunt.registerTask('default', 'mochaTest');
};
```

The preceding Gruntfile loads the grunt-mocha-test plug-in and uses it to operate on all files in the `test` folder that have the extension `.js`. To match on all files within the test directory, we've used a wildcard pattern. The pattern used will match all files within the top-level test directory and any subdirectories of it. If we wished only to match on files within the top-level test folder, we could simplify our pattern to `*.js`. The important thing to note here is the lack of a `dest` property, as a task does not output to a file.

File Object Format

The file object format allows for multiple source-destination file mappings. The file object format declares the mapping as a JavaScript object wherein the destination is the property key, while the value can be one or more source files. As each mapping is essentially keyed by the "destination" file, there can be many mappings per target. This format is commonly used when you want to reduce a set of files into a single file, such as in the case of concatenating JavaScript.

The following Gruntfile (Listing 2-17) demonstrates the use of the file object format.

Listing 2-17. Using the File Object Format to Concatenate Files

```
module.exports = function(grunt) {

  // Project configuration.
  grunt.initConfig({
    pkg: grunt.file.readJSON('package.json'),

    concat: {
      options: {
        separator: ';',
      },
```

```
      dist: {
        files: {
          'build/app.js': ['src/fileA.js', 'src/fileB.js']
        }
      }
    }
  });

  // Load the plugin that provides the "concat" task.
  grunt.loadNpmTasks('grunt-contrib-concat');
};
```

The preceding Gruntfile revisits our earlier example, but instead of defining `src` and `dest` properties, the destination file is defined as the property name itself.

Files Array Format

The files array format extends the compact format by allowing multiple source-destination mappings per target. Instead of taking a single `src` and `dest` property, the files are declared as a `files` property, and the value of this property is an array of the compact format. The following example (Listing 2-18) modifies our existing example by adding CSS concatenation into the same target.

Listing 2-18. Use File Array Format to Concatentate Multiple Files Together

```
module.exports = function(grunt) {

  // Project configuration.
  grunt.initConfig({
    pkg: grunt.file.readJSON('package.json'),

    concat: {
      options: {
        separator: ';',
      },
      dist: {
        files: [
          {src: ['src/fileA.js', 'src/fileB.js'], dest: 'build/app.js'},
          {src: ['src/stylesA.css', 'src/stylesB.css'], dest: 'build/app.css'}
        ]
      }
    }
  });

  // Load the plugin that provides the "concat" task.
  grunt.loadNpmTasks('grunt-contrib-concat');
};
```

In the preceding example, the `src` and `dest` properties have been replaced with a `files` property. The `files` property is assigned an array of objects. Each object has `src` and `dest` properties, allowing multiple source-destination mappings to be declared. The output for the `dist` target will be `build/app.js` and `build/app.css`.

Summary

In this chapter, you've begun to explore how we can introduce Grunt into a project. You started by becoming familiar with Node and npm, as these are fundamental to understanding how Grunt and its plug-in ecosystem work. The remainder of this chapter discussed installing Grunt into a project, how to install our first task, and how to provide the required configuration for the task. Finally, the flexible API that Grunt provides for pattern matching files within our project, to define inputs and outputs for our tasks, was introduced.

The next chapter will begin to look at real-world use cases for employing Grunt to automate common tasks associated with HTML and CSS.

CHAPTER 3

Using Grunt with HTML and CSS

In the previous chapter, we explored how to bootstrap a project to use Grunt and how to install and configure tasks within a project. Next, we'll look at a variety of useful plug-ins that can help with our workflow when working with HTML and CSS, the fundamentals of the Web. The topics covered in this chapter include CSS preprocessing, simplifying installation of third-party dependencies, and optimizing content for release to the public.

Before we explore the tasks available to automate while working with HTML and CSS, let me introduce the project we'll use to demonstrate all the fantastic plug-ins available.

The Demo App

Throughout the remainder of the book, we will look at a variety of Grunt plug-ins that are freely available for you to use on future projects. To help demonstrate each of these plug-ins, we develop an application. This application will be a simple Node application that allows users to keep a simple to-do list in the browser. There is no need to worry if you have little experience with Node, as we'll be using Node to run a very simple web server.

The vast majority of the application will be HTML, CSS, and JavaScript. To start, let's use a stripped-down version of the HTML5 boilerplate HTML (see Listing 3-1).

Listing 3-1. HTML Boilerplate for the To-Do List App

```
<!DOCTYPE html>
<html class="no-js">
 <head>
  <meta charset="utf-8">
  <meta http-equiv="X-UA-Compatible" content="IE=edge">
  <title>Pro Grunt.js: Todo List</title>
  <meta name="description" content="">
  <meta name="viewport" content="width=device-width, initial-scale=1">

  <link rel="stylesheet" href="css/main.css">
 </head>
 <body>
  <!--[if lt IE 8]>
   <p class="browsehappy">You are using an <strong>outdated</strong> browser. Please <a
href="http://browsehappy.com/">upgrade your browser</a> to improve your experience.</p>
  <![endif]-->
```

```
  <!-- Add your site or application content here -->
  <h1>Pro Grunt.js</h1>
  <h2>Todo List</h2>

  <script src="//ajax.googleapis.com/ajax/libs/jquery/1.11.0/jquery.min.js"></script>
  <script>window.jQuery || document.write('<script src="js/vendor/jquery-1.11.0.min.js">
<\/script>')</script>
  <script src="js/main.js"></script>
 </body>
</html>
```

As you can see from Listing 3-1, the HTML document is very small at present. There is a CSS file included in the head element; jQuery and main.js JavaScript files are included at the end of the body tag. For now, don't worry about the CSS and JavaScript files, as this will be covered later in the book. First let's see how Grunt can help generate, lint, and minify our CSS file.

CSS Preprocessing

CSS preprocessing is a relatively new technology, existing only for approximately the past five years. Within these five years, there has been rapid adoption by developers, primarily owing to it solving some of the pain points of using CSS. As it stands, there are currently three major CSS preproccesors available: LESS (`http://lesscss.org`), Sass (`http://sass-lang.com`), and Stylus (`www.stylus.com`). CSS preprocessors have grown in such popularity that browser vendors have started to offer support as part of their developer tools.

CSS preprocessors typically extend CSS, offering new features such as the ability to define variables and nested selectors. This generally leads to cleaner and more maintainable CSS. For demonstration purposes, in this book, we will be using Sass. To use Sass, you must have the Ruby language installed.

Installing Sass

To be able to install Sass, you will have to install Ruby onto your machine. Once successfully installed, Ruby should be available via the command line or command prompt.

Installing Ruby on Linux

To install Ruby on Linux, it is best to install it from your distribution package manager or tools such as rbenv or rvm.

Installing Ruby on Windows

On Windows, there is a one-click installer for Ruby. Once installed, Ruby should be available on the command prompt.

Installing Ruby on Mac OS X

Ruby comes preinstalled on Mac OS X; however, the version install depends on the version of Mac OS X you are running. Mountain Lion comes bundled with version 1.8.7, while Mavericks comes with Ruby 2.0.0.

I would recommend running 2.0.0 while working with Sass. For those readers using Mountain Lion or older versions, I'd recommend using rbenv to install and maintain your Ruby installations.

Checking Your Ruby Installation

Once you have Ruby installed, you should be able to run the Ruby command from the command line or command prompt. Listing 3-2 demonstrates how to check which version of Ruby you have installed.

Listing 3-2. Checking the Version of Ruby Installed

```
ruby --version
```

This command should output something similar to what is shown in Figure 3-1.

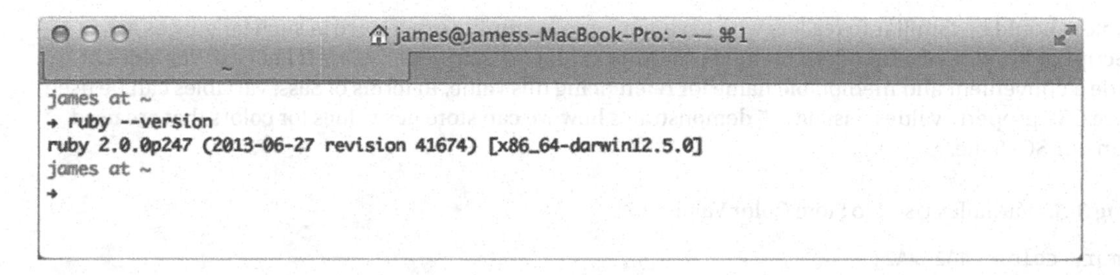

Figure 3-1. *Ruby version currently installed*

If you do not see a similar output to the one above, I would recommend double-checking the installation steps for the platform you are running. To get started with Sass, the next step is to install the gem. Similar to Node, Ruby has a package manager system called Ruby Gems, and each Ruby package is bundled as a gem. Listing 3-3 demonstrates how to install Sass from the command line or command prompt and subsequently check the version of Sass installed.

Listing 3-3. Installing Sass Gem

```
gem install sass
sass --version
```

If Sass has successfully installed, a similar output to `Sass 3.3.3 (Maptastic Maple)` will be printed. Now that we have Sass installed, let's take a brief look at its key features, before looking at how Grunt can help us while working with Sass.

Brief Introduction to Sass

As mentioned earlier, Sass is a CSS preproccessor. You're probably wondering what this means. Well, Sass takes some input, runs a process over it, and the output is CSS. By this process, the input can either be SCSS or Sass files. SCSS is the main syntax of Sass 3, and what we will be using throughout this book. Sass is a slightly older syntax-inspired HAML that has a much stricter set of rules for compiling.

The SCSS, also known as Sassy CSS, is a superset of CSS3, which means that any CSS3 style sheet is a valid SCSS style sheet. SCSS files have the file extension `.scss`. Listing 3-4 demonstrates how Sass can be used to compile a SCSS file to CSS from the command line.

Listing 3-4. Compiling an SCSS File to CSS Using Sass

```
sass input.scss output.css
```

Running the command in Listing 3-4 will output a CSS file containing all the styles listed in the SCSS file `input.scss`. The command-like tool `sass` can also be passed a number of flags to modify the generated CSS file. We will take a look at some of these flags later in the chapter. Before this, we'll explore the features of Sass that improve the maintainability and readability of our CSS files.

Variables

Variables should be familiar to readers who have some programming experience in such languages as JavaScript or Ruby. Variables offer a method of storing a value so that we can reuse it later on. Variables also provide a convenient and memorable name for referencing this value. In terms of Sass, variables can be used to store CSS property values. Listing 3-5 demonstrates how we can store hex values for colors that are used later in our SCSS file.

Listing 3-5. Variables Used to Store Color Values

```
$primary-color: #A2A2A2;
$background-color: #C3C3C3;

body {
    color: $primary-color;
    background: $background-color;
}
```

Variables start with `$` and then name of the variable. The value of the variable appears after the `:`. In our example, we're only using variables to store color values, but variables can also store CSS attribute values for any CSS property. When Sass is processing, the variables are replaced with the variable values, but the variable definitions are not. Listing 3-6 shows the preceding example after it has been processed.

Listing 3-6. CSS Output from Processing the SCSS File in Listing 3-5

```
body {
    color: #A2A2A2;
    background: #C3C3C3;
}
```

Nesting

Another powerful feature is the ability to nest selectors, which allows CSS authors to nest their CSS selectors to match the visual representation of your HTML. Listing 3-7 demonstrates how nesting can be used to make your CSS more readable and maintainable.

Listing 3-7. Using Nested Selectors

```
header {
    width: 936px;
    padding: 12px;

    h1 {
         font-size: 2.4em;
         line-height: 1em;
         margin: 0 0 12px;
    }

    nav {
        padding: 12px;
    }
}
```

Note how the `h1` and `nav` selectors are nested within the header selector. As Sass processes the SCSS file, it collapses nested selectors to generate more complex selectors. The output from the SCSS file in Listing 3-7 is shown in Listing 3-8.

Listing 3-8. Output from Nested Selectors

```
header {
    width: 936px;
    padding: 12px;
}

header h1 {
    font-size: 2.4em;
    line-height: 1em;
    margin: 0 0 12px;
}

header nav {
    padding: 12px;
}
```

In addition to nesting selectors, a more advanced feature is available to combine nested pseudo-class selectors (as shown in Listing 3-9).

Listing 3-9. Pseudo-class Selectors Combined with Nested Selectors

```
a {
    text-decoration: none;

    &:hover,
    &:focus {
        text-decoration: underline;
    }
}
```

Note the use of the ampersand (&) in Listing 3-9. This leads to the current selector being appended to the parent selector, which in our example is a. The output of our example is shown in Listing 3-10, with the selector `a:hover, a:focus` being generated.

Listing 3-10. Appending Pseudo-class Selectors with &

```
a {
    text-decoration: none;
}

a:hover, a:focus {
     text-decoration: underline;
}
```

Partials and Imports

Partials allow developers to create SCSS files that contain a snippet of CSS. These snippets can then be included in other SCSS files. The ability to include other snippets into other SCSS files dramatically improves the reuse of the SCSS you write, as you can pick and choose which partials to include. Partials have a file name convention that means they must begin with an underscore. This tells Sass that the file does not directly generate output. For example, a partial for the header module might be named `_header.scss`.

To include partials within a file, you have to use the `@import` directive. Imports, coupled with partials, allow you to split your CSS into more manageable and readable chunks. Listing 3-11 illustrates how the `@import` directive can be used.

Listing 3-11. Using the `@import` Directive to Combine Multiple Files with Sass

```
// _reset.scss

html, body, ul, ol, h1, h2, h3, h4, h5, h5, p {
    margin: 0;
    padding: 0;
}

// _header.scss

header {
    h1 {
        font-size: 2em;
        margin: 12px 0;
    }
}

// main.scss

@import 'reset';
@import 'header';

body {
    color: #A2A2A2;
    background: #C3C3C3;
}
```

In Listing 3-11, there are a total of three files: `_reset.scss`, `_header.scss`, and `main.scss`. The `main.scss` file imports the contents of the `_reset.scss` and `_header.scss` files. It is important to note that when using the `@import` directive, you must include the file extension `.scss`. When Sass processes `main.scss`, it will generate a single file, not three. The `@import` directive in Sass should not be confused with the `@import` directive from CSS. These provide very different functionality. When using the `@import` directive in Sass, the contents of the file merge into the files that import the partial. With CSS imports, each file remains separate, and the browser makes a separate HTTP call for each file. Listing 3-12 shows the output from compiling the `main.scss` file.

Listing 3-12. Output from Compiling Sass with Imports and Partials

```
html, body, ul, ol, h1, h2, h3, h4, h5, h5, p {
    margin: 0;
    padding: 0;
}

header {
    h1 {
        font-size: 2em;
        margin: 12px 0;
    }
}

body {
    color: #A2A2A2;
    background: #C3C3C3;
}
```

Mixins

Mixins provide a method to reuse CSS in a convenient way that allows you to define a set of selectors or properties and reuse them multiple times without copying and pasting them. In addition to this, mixins can also accept parameters, so that each time they are used, they can be slightly altered to meet specific needs. The primary benefit of mixins is the improved maintainability, because if you have to update the CSS later, you only have to modify it in a single place. A common example of the use of mixins is browser prefixes. Instead of having to continually define each browser vendor's particular implementation, you can capture this in a single mixin. This means that if the browser vendor changes its implementation, you only have to modify the mixin, and the rest of the CSS output will be updated with the change. Listing 3-13 demonstrates such an example with the CSS3 property `border-radius`.

Listing 3-13. Defining a Sass Mixin for the CSS3 Property `border-radius`

```
@mixin border-radius($radius) {
    -webkit-border-radius: $radius;
    -moz-border-radius: $radius;
    -ms-border-radius: $radius;
    border-radius: $radius;
}
```

```
.panel {
  @include border-radius(4px);
}

.login-box {
  @include border-radius(10px);
}
```

In Listing 3-13, we define a mixin with the name `border-radius` and then use the mixin by applying it to the class selector `panel`. The mixin starts with the directive `@mixin`, followed by the name and a set of parameters. In our example, there is a single parameter, `radius`, which is a Sass variable, so it begins with $. Using a parameter in this mixin allows us to pass in the radius to be applied to our selector. To use a mixin, the `@include` directive is used. The `@include` is followed by the mixin's name and a set of parameters, if required. Listing 3-14 illustrates the output from the Sass in Listing 3-13.

Listing 3-14. CSS Output from Using Mixins

```
.panel {
    -webkit-border-radius: 4px;
    -moz-border-radius: 4px;
    -ms-border-radius: 4px;
    border-radius: 4px;
}

.login-box {
  -webkit-border-radius: 10px;
  -moz-border-radius: 10px;
  -ms-border-radius: 10px;
  border-radius: 10px;
}
```

It should be noted that a mixin itself is not output in the CSS, only the use of the mixin where it has been included.

Extend/Inheritance

The final Sass feature we'll look at in this introduction is inheritance. Inheritance allows you to keep your CSS DRY. For those unfamiliar with the principle of DRY, it stands for "Don't Repeat Yourself" and aims to reduce repetition. Sass provides the ability to keep our CSS DRY through the directive `@extend`. Listing 3-15 demonstrates how to use `@extend`.

Listing 3-15. Using `@extend` to Keep CSS Output DRY

```
.notice {
    border: 1px solid #FBCE2D;
    padding: 8px;
}

.alert {
    @extend .notice;
    border-color: #F0F0F0;
}
```

In Listing 3-15, we define the class selectors `.notice` and `.alert`. The `@extend` directive is used as part of the `.alert` property definitions, with the name of the selector we want to extend. As part of the CSS generation, the `.notice` and `.alert` selectors are combined into a rule. This can be seen in Listing 3-16.

Listing 3-16. Output from Use of `@extend`

```
.notice, .alert {
    border: 1px solid #FBCE2D;
    padding: 8px;
}

.alert {
    border-color: #F0F0F0;
}
```

Now that we've seen the power that Sass can offer in terms of making working with large and complex style sheets easier, let's look at how Grunt can help us speed up our workflow.

Sass with Grunt

To compile your Sass files with Grunt, a Grunt plug-in called grunt-contrib-sass is available. Plug-ins that begin with "grunt-contrib" are plug-ins officially supported by the core Grunt team. To install this plug-in, follow the same procedure as introduced in the previous chapter. (See Listing 3-17).

Listing 3-17. Installing grunt-contrib-sass

```
npm install grunt-contrib-sass --save-dev
```

At this point, grunt-contrib-sass has been added to our project, and the dependency added to our `package.json` file. Next, we have to add the task to our Gruntfile. Listing 3-18 demonstrates our Gruntfile with the newly added plug-in configured to compile our Sass.

Listing 3-18. Gruntfile Configured with grunt-contrib-sass

```
/*global module:false*/
module.exports = function(grunt) {

  // Project configuration.
  grunt.initConfig({

    // Task configuration.
    sass: {
      dist: {
        options: {
          style: 'expanded'
        },
        files: {
          'css/main.css': 'build/styles/main.scss'
        }
      }
    }
  });
```

```
  // These plugins provide necessary tasks.
  grunt.loadNpmTasks('grunt-contrib-sass');

  // Default task.
  grunt.registerTask('default', ['sass']);
};
```

The Gruntfile in Listing 3-18 should look fairly familiar to the one we used in the previous chapter. The `grunt-contrib-sass` task is loaded toward the end of the file, and the `sass` task is set as the default task. The rest of the Grunt file is taken up by the configuration for the task. We've added a target called `dist`, and inside this, we've set one option, `style`. The `grunt-contrib-sass` task wraps the Sass command and exposes some of the flags that the Sass command accepts to alter the CSS output.

The `style` option modifies the format of the CSS that is output. There are four possible values for this option: `nested`, `expanded`, `compact`, and `compressed`. The default value is `nested`, which indents the CSS similarly to the Sass files. The expanded value is the most verbose and looks similar to the handwritten CSS. This style is great when trying to work out difficult CSS issues locally. `compact` and `compressed` styles, as their names suggest, are smaller formats. `compact` style outputs each selector on a single line along with all CSS properties and values for the selector. `compressed` processes the minimal output. All whitespace is removed, except for the space required for each selector. With the `compress` style, all selectors appear on the same line, and this is ideal for using on your live site. In addition to the style options, grunt-contribub-sass provides options for outputting source line numbers in the CSS output, either to cache the compiled sass or produce a source map. I'll be covering source maps later in this book, as part of advanced topics.

The final part of our Sass Gruntfile configuration defines the files to use. In this case, we've opted to use the file object format to configure which files are used for the task. As you can see, we're using the SCSS file `main.scss` in the path of `build/styles`. It should be noted that this is relative to the Gruntfile. Let's take our Gruntfile for a spin. Fire up the command line and navigate to the project space. Running Grunt at this point should output something similar to what is shown in Figure 3-2.

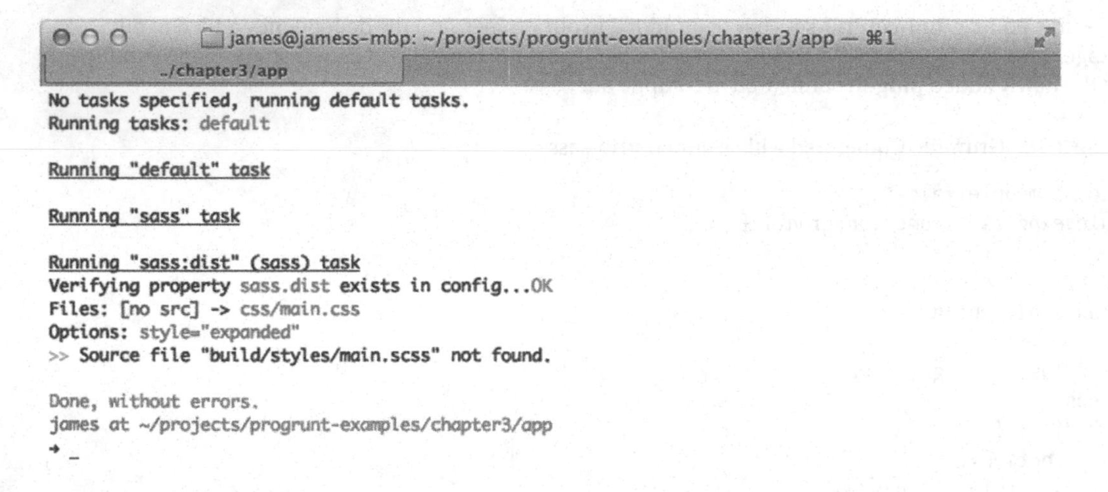

Figure 3-2. *Failing Sass Grunt configuration, due to lack of source file*

As you can see, Grunt fails, with an error message informing us that the source file cannot be found. Add the file folder `styles`. This folder should be inside the `build` folder. Rerunning Grunt will now complete successfully, with the message "File css/main.css created." If you open the `application` folder, you should now see that there is a `css` folder created and `main.css` within it. Listing 3-19 illustrates the project structure at this stage.

Listing 3-19. `main.scss` for Our Demo Application

```
$primary-color: #a2a2a2;

body {
  color: $primary-color;
}
```

At this stage, our to-do application looks very basic—with a mere title. Let's start to pack some functionality and spruce up the styles by pulling in some libraries to help us. In the next section, you will see how Grunt can help simplify importing libraries into our projects.

Working with Front-End Frameworks with Grunt

Over the past few years, there has been an increase in demand for web applications to offer the same rich immersive that native applications provide. To meet this demand, web applications have become increasing complex. With this increase in complexity, we've seen the emergence of powerful front-end frameworks to aid developers to quickly prototype and deliver new features for these web applications. This has introduced a new challenge: how, as developers, we install and manage these dependencies. Back-end technologies, such as Ruby and Java, have had dependency manager tools to solve this problem for some time. Thankfully, there is now a solution for front-end libraries too, in the form of a tool called Bower, from Twitter. Before looking at how we can integrate Bower with Grunt, let's find out a little more about Bower itself.

Bower

Bower is a package manager built for the Web that aims to solve the problem of front-end package management. Bower, like npm, does not install package-wide; instead, packages are isolated to a local project. This is extremely useful if you have to work across multiple projects and do not want to share dependencies. Packages are installed via Git; however, the contents of each package may vary, as Bower does not dictate what a package should contain. For example, a package may contain JavaScript or CSS, or any other type of asset, for that matter.

Installing Bower

Bower, like npm, depends on Node. Listing 3-20 demonstrates how to install `bower`. This should be fairly familiar to you at this point.

Listing 3-20. Installing Bower

```
npm install -g bower
```

Note that we use the `-g` flag to install `bower`, as Bower is accessed via the command line. After the installation process is completed, Bower should now be available via the command line. To check its availability, you can run the command shown in Listing 3-21.

Listing 3-21. Checking the Version of Bower Installed

```
bower --version
```

In addition to installing Bower, you will also have to have Git installed. The Git web site offers some great installation instructions for each platform (`http://git-scm.com/book/en/Getting-Started-Installing-Git`).

Using Bower

Bower has a very simple set of commands to manage dependency. These include installing, searching, and uninstalling packages. Bower has a few methods for installing packages. First, Bower can read a configuration file known as `bower.json`. `bower.json` is akin to `package.json`, as it defines a project's front-end dependences, while `package.json` defines Node dependencies for a project. Listing 3-22 provides a sample `bower.json` and the command required to install the dependencies using `bower.json`.

Listing 3-22. `bower.json` and Installing Dependencies

```
// bower.json
{
  "name": "todo-app",
  "dependencies": {
    "jquery": "~2.1.0"
  }
}

bower install
```

With the preceding file saved in the root of your project, you run the `bower install` command. This will then either look for jQuery locally or remotely. Once found, the package is downloaded and installed into a folder named `bower_components`. With the `bower_components` folder, each package is contained with the folder. We shall see shortly how to control which folder `bower` uses for installing packages. Before this, let's continue with the various methods of installing packages. Listing 3-23 demonstrates how to install a package by passing the package name and saving the dependency to the `bower.json` file automatically.

Listing 3-23. `bower.json` and Installing Dependencies

```
bower install backbone -S
```

This will install the popular JavaScript MVC framework Backbone.js (`http://backbonejs.org/`) into the `bower_components` folder. As the Backbone.js package defines a dependency on the library Underscore.js, Bower also installs this for us as part of the single command. Listing 3-24 shows the `bower.json` file after the command from Listing 3-23 has completed successfully.

Listing 3-24. `bower.json` after Install Backbone.js

```
{
  "name": "todo-app",
  "dependencies": {
    "jquery": "~2.1.0",
    "backbone": "~1.1.2"
  }
}
```

In the preceding example, the Bower package is installed by the package's name. However, this can be replaced with a URL for the Git repository, svn repository, zip file, or tar file.

In addition to install packages, Bower offers the ability to search for packages via the command line. Figure 3-3 shows a sample search for Twitter Bootstrap. Matching results contain the package name and the URL that the package is available from.

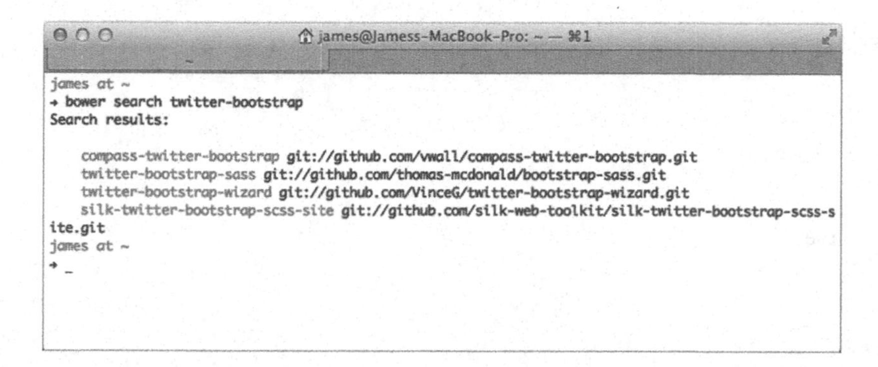

Figure 3-3. *Using Bower to search for front-end packages*

As mentioned previously, the folder in which Bower installs packages can be controlled by settings within your `.bowerrc` file. Listing 3-25 demonstrates how to modify the folder by showing the contents of a `.bowerrc` file. The `.bowerrc` file should be saved in the root of the project, alongside the `bower.json` file.

Listing 3-25. `bowerrc` File to Install Bower Packages to a Specific Folder

```
{
  "directory": "build/bower_components"
}
```

Running the `bower install` command will not lead to components being installed into the `build` folder.

This concludes the brief introduction to Bower. It is an extremely powerful tool that can help when working with lots of front-end frameworks. Next you will see how we can use Grunt and Bower to automate insertion of the Bower components into our page as they are installed.

Bower with Grunt

Bower is an amazing tool without Grunt, but when used together, it can dramatically reduce the time required to scaffold your front-end dependencies. The plug-in that bridges the gap between Bower and Grunt is called grunt-bower-install. The grunt-bower-install plug-in can be used to automate the injection of front-end JavaScript and CSS files that have been installed by Bower into your HTML. To achieve this, grunt-bower-install relies on wiredep, a Node module. When wiredep is run over your source files, it looks for special comments in the HTML. If it finds a comment, it will inject the relevant tag into the HTML.

First, let's update the Gruntfile.js to use the new plug-in. Don't forget that you'll also have to install this plug-in. Listing 3-26 shows the updated Grunt file with the task added.

Listing 3-26. bowerrc File to Install Bower Packages to a Specific Folder

```
/*global module:false*/
module.exports = function(grunt) {

  // Project configuration.
  grunt.initConfig({
    // Task configuration.
    ...

    bowerInstall: {
      dist: {
        src: ['*.html'],
        dependencies: true,
        devDependencies: true,
        exclude: []
      }
    }
  });

  // These plugins provide necessary tasks.
  grunt.loadNpmTasks('grunt-contrib-sass');
  grunt.loadNpmTasks('grunt-bower-install');

  // Default task.
  grunt.registerTask('default', ['sass', 'bower-install']);
};
```

Listing 3-26 introduces a new task, `bowerInstall`, with a target of `dist`. This target has a number of options, the first being the `src`. The grunt-bower-install plug-in updates the HTML; therefore, it does not require a destination file. The next two options determine which dependencies should be injected into the HTML. Dependencies are the production and development dependences, while devDependencies relates to Bower packages that are only required for development. The final option is `exclude`, which is empty in our example but can be used to exclude particular libraries from being processed by the plug-in. A number of additional options are available for this plug-in, including the ability to inject imports into Sass files.

Before running the task on the project, there is one final step: updating the HTML. Listing 3-27 contains the HTML file that we first saw at the start of the chapter, but with jQuery removed from the footer. In place of jQuery, a new comment has been added for wiredep to use while processing the HTML file.

Listing 3-27. HTML Modifications to Support the grunt-bower-install Plug-in

```
<!doctype html>
<html class="no-js">
<head>
<meta charset="utf-8">
<meta http-equiv="X-UA-Compatible" content="IE=edge">
<title>Pro Grunt.js: Todo List</title>
<meta name="description" content="">
<meta name="viewport" content="width=device-width, initial-scale=1">
```

```
<!-- bower:css -->
<!-- endbower -->
<link rel="stylesheet" href="css/main.css">

</head>
<body>
    <!--[if lt IE 8]>
    <p class="browsehappy">You are using an <strong>outdated</strong> browser. Please <a
href="http://browsehappy.com/">upgrade your browser</a> to improve your experience.</p>
    <![endif]-->

    <!-- Add your site or application content here -->
    <h1>Pro Grunt.js</h1>
    <h2>Todo List</h2>

    <!-- bower:js -->
    <!-- endbower -->
    <script src="js/main.js"></script>
</body>
</html>
```

The comments added before the final script tag at the end of the body is a placeholder for wiredep to inject references to the Bower components into the outputted HTML file. To run the task, use the command shown in Listing 3-28.

Listing 3-28. Running grunt-bower-install

```
grunt bowerInstall
```

As the task runs it should notify of any files that it is update as it runs. In our example, this should be the `index.html` file. Once the task has completed, if you open the `index.html` file, references to jQuery, Backbone.js, and Underscore.js will have been added between the `bower. js` comments. Listing 3-29 contains a snippet of the HTML after the task has run.

Listing 3-29. `index.html` Snippet after Grunt Task

```
<!-- bower:js -->
<script src="build/bower_components/jquery/dist/jquery.js"></script>
<script src="build/bower_components/underscore/underscore.js"></script>
<script src="build/bower_components/backbone/backbone.js"></script>
<!-- endbower -->
```

At this point, this might not appear that useful, but imagine a scenario in which you return to a project three months from now. There is a new framework you want to use for your project. It takes two commands to download and inject the framework into our page.

Linting

So far, we've seen how to generate CSS and import third-party libraries. Both the tasks generate some output or modify a file within your project. In this section, you will see how Grunt can provide tools to validate our HTML and CSS to adhere to a common set of rules.

Although there is a strong feeling in the developer community that HTML validation has lost some relevance as browser vendors strive to implement the latest features before they are finalized in an official standard that can complicate validation, this should not prevent teams from having a baseline standard for both HTML and CSS. A team with a solid set of standards can get new members on board more quickly, as they have a set of rules to follow, and the current HTML and CSS follow a similar pattern.

Setting a Standard for Your CSS

Let's introduce another tool from the Twitter team, RECESS. RECESS is a Node command line, too, that can either lint or build your CSS from LESS files. RECESS will check your CSS to ensure that styles are tidy and consistent. It applies a number of rules against your CSS while linting is performed. Following is a list of these rules:

- *No IDs*: The CSS should not contain ID selectors.
- *No JS Prefixes*: The CSS should not contain class selectors with `.js-` prepended.
- *No over qualifying of selectors*: The CSS should not contain selectors that have been overqualified, for example, `div#home.page`.
- *No underscores*: CSS class selectors should not have class names that contain underscores.
- *No universal selectors*: CSS should not contain a selector of *.
- *No zeros with units*: CSS should not contain attribute values of zero that have an associated unit. For example, `padding: 0px;` would be invalid. Instead, this should be `padding: 0`.
- *Strict property order*: CSS should conform to RECESS property order.

RECESS is available as a standalone Node command-like tool. However, there is already a Grunt plug-in that wraps the Node tool so that CSS linting can be automated. The name of the Grunt plug-in is grunt-recess. Listing 3-30 shows the project Gruntfile modified to include RECESS.

Listing 3-30. Gruntfile Modified to Include RECESS

```
/*global module:false*/
module.exports = function(grunt) {

  // Project configuration.
  grunt.initConfig({
    // Task configuration.
    ...
    recess: {
      dist: {
        options: {
          compile: false,
          noIDs: true
        },
```

```
        files: {
          'src': 'css/main.css',
        }
      }
    });

    // These plugins provide necessary tasks.
    grunt.loadNpmTasks('grunt-bower-install');
    grunt.loadNpmTasks('grunt-contrib-sass');
    grunt.loadNpmTasks('grunt-recess');

    // Default task.
    grunt.registerTask('default', ['sass', 'bower-install', 'recess']);

};
```

In the preceding Gruntfile, the task for RECESS has been added with some new configuration. To keep it in line with our other tasks, we've defined a target of `dist`. For this target, we've set the `compile` option to `false`. RECESS is able to compile LESS and CSS, restructuring rules in line with its rules. As we're generating our CSS from Sass, this option has been set to `false`. The other option set is `noIDs`. This relates back to the set of rules RECESS applies. Setting `noIDs` to `true` will lead to RECESS reporting invalid CSS if the CSS contains an ID selector. This is shown in Figure 3-4.

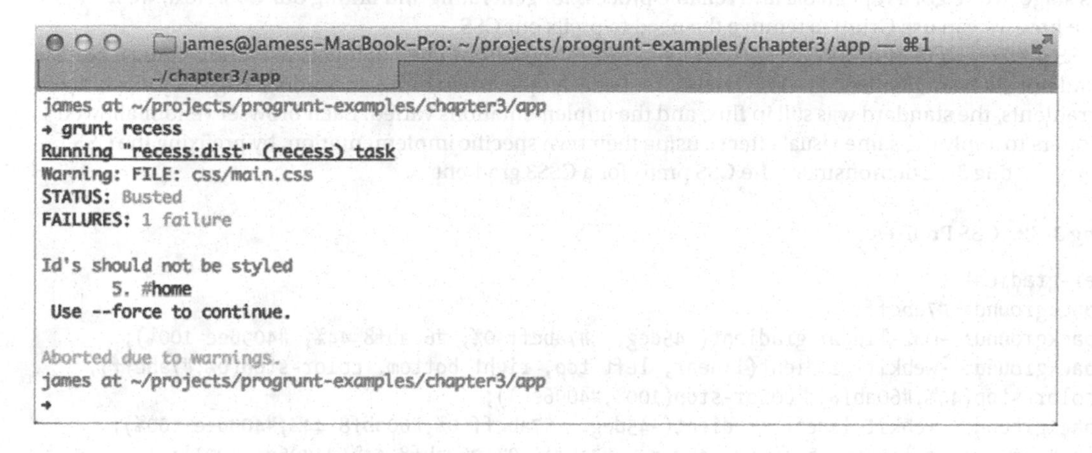

Figure 3-4. *Failing RECESS task due to ID selectors*

The remainder of the configuration defines the file we want RECESS to process. As this task does not generate a file output, we only have to define a source file and no destination. With the addition of this task, each time we run the `grunt` command, our Sass will be compiled with the CSS being output to `css/main.css`. After this, RECESS will process our CSS to ensure it is tidy and consistent.

Currently, the RECESS task is looking for a single CSS file. However, Grunt has the ability to use wildcards within file paths, to match many files. Listing 3-31 demonstrates how to use wildcards within the file paths.

Listing 3-31. Using Wildcards to Match Multiple CSS Files

```
recess: {
  dist: {
    options: {
      compile: false,
      noIDs: true
    },
    files: {
      'src': 'css/**/*.css',
  }
}
```

By making this small change, outlined in Listing 3-31, we can add more CSS files to the css folder. In addition to adding extra CSS files to this css folder, we can add folders that contain CSS files, and Grunt will process these as well.

I hope, at this point, that you can begin to see how we can use different tasks together to produce a repeatable process for the whole team to use.

Prefixing

At this stage, we've got a repeatable and reliable process for generating and linting our CSS. Next, we'll explore how we can use Grunt to remove the need to prefix our CSS.

CSS prefixes were introduced by browser vendors to allow front-end engineers to use emerging features that had not yet been finalized in a W3C standard. For example, when browser vendors originally introduced CSS gradients, the standard was still in flux, and the implementations varied. Each browser vendor allowed developers to apply the same visual effects, using their own specific implementation, by prefixing the CSS property. Listing 3-32 demonstrates the CSS prefix for a CSS3 gradient.

Listing 3-32. CSS Prefixes

```
.super-gradient {
    background: #7abcff;
    background: -moz-linear-gradient(-45deg,  #7abcff 0%, #60abf8 44%, #4096ee 100%);
    background: -webkit-gradient(linear, left top, right bottom, color-stop(0%,#7abcff),
    color-stop(44%,#60abf8), color-stop(100%,#4096ee));
    background: -webkit-linear-gradient(-45deg,  #7abcff 0%,#60abf8 44%,#4096ee 100%);
    background: -o-linear-gradient(-45deg,  #7abcff 0%,#60abf8 44%,#4096ee 100%);
    background: -ms-linear-gradient(-45deg,  #7abcff 0%,#60abf8 44%,#4096ee 100%);
    background: linear-gradient(135deg,  #7abcff 0%,#60abf8 44%,#4096ee 100%);
}
```

Listing 3-32 demonstrates different implementations of linear CSS gradients, in particular, the difference between FireFox (prefixed with -moz) and webkit (prefixed with -webkit). As you may have noticed, there is a lot of repetition in the preceding CSS. Some developers in the community are against the use of prefixes, as they can contribute to bloated CSS, as each property must be repeated for each browser, which can easily bloat the CSS required for a site.

To solve the first issue, the repetition, there is a tool called autoprefixer. You can probably guess what it does by the name, but to clarify, autoprefixer parses CSS and adds vendor-specific prefixes to CSS rules using values from the popular site Can I Use (http://caniuse.com/). Autoprefixer is a Node application that can be installed using npm or integrated to other Node applications to be used programmatically. Listing 3-33 shows how the autoprefixer can be used on the command line.

Listing 3-33. Autoprefixer on the Command Line

```
autoprefixer styles/main.css
```

The preceding command will parse the CSS style sheet and add vendor-specific prefixes to the same file. The example in Listing 3-34 demonstrates a before and after view.

Listing 3-34. Before and After View of CSS When Using Autoprefixer

```
/* Before */

h1 {
  box-sizing: border-box;
}

/* After */

h1 {
  -webkit-box-sizing: border-box;
  -moz-box-sizing: border-box;
  box-sizing: border-box;
}
```

As you can see from Listing 3-34, autoprefixer can save a lot of time, as it will add in the vendor-specific rules. Another benefit of using autoprefixer is the reduced need to learn every vendor's specific implementations for new features. In addition to these two benefits, autoprefixer is kept up to date as it uses the Can I Use site, reducing the need to track changes in browser implementations. Next, we'll take a look at a plug-in that can automate the prefixing of our CSS.

There is a Grunt plug-in that wraps the Node module to run autoprefixer via Grunt. The name of the plug-in is grunt-autoprefixer. Listing 3-35 demonstrates the new task in the Gruntfile.

Listing 3-35. Grunt Task

```
/*global module:false*/
module.exports = function(grunt) {

  // Project configuration.
  grunt.initConfig({
  ...
    autoprefixer: {
      dist: {
        options: {
           diff: true
        },
        src: 'css/main.css',
      },
    }
  });
```

```
    // These plugins provide necessary tasks.
    grunt.loadNpmTasks('grunt-contrib-sass');
    grunt.loadNpmTasks('grunt-bower-install');
    grunt.loadNpmTasks('grunt-recess');
    grunt.loadNpmTasks('grunt-autoprefixer');

    // Default task.
    grunt.registerTask('default', ['sass', 'bowerInstall', 'recess', 'autoprefixer']);

};
```

After installing the Grunt plug-in, grunt-autoprefixer, and applying the preceding Gruntfile to your project, you will have the autoprefixing automated. Each time you run Grunt, the CSS produced will be parsed to autoprefixer for vendor-specific prefixes to be added. In our configuration, we also define the option `diff` and set this to `true`. When autoprefixer modifies your CSS, it can be told to generate a patch file that contains the difference between the source CSS and the CSS produced by autoprefixer. In addition to this, autoprefixer can be configured to target specific browsers when generating the vendor prefixes. These can be passed to the Grunt task via options.

As mentioned previously, prefixing can sometimes be frowned upon, as it can lead to bloated CSS. In the next section, we will look at Grunt tasks that can automate minifying our HTML and CSS to improve the performance of a project.

Minification

Performance of web applications should be a concern for every developer. As a developer, it is your responsibility to ensure you've done your best to optimize your application. One of the key factors that can affect the loading performance of a web application is the size of the assets within the page. For example, large CSS or JavaScript files can lead to poor performance, as it takes longer for the browser to download, which ultimately can block the browser from initially rendering the page. Therefore, it is the responsibility of the developer(s) of the application to ensure that assets delivered in their live system are optimized.

The goal of minification is always to preserve the operational qualities of the code while reducing its overall byte footprint. In this context, minifying HTML and CSS means reducing the size of the content for each resource by stripping unnecessary content. If we look at CSS, there are a number of modifications by which its size can be reduced.

- Removing comments
- Removing whitespace
- Removing the last semicolon in a declaration block
- Removing additional semicolons
- Reducing zero values
- Stripping leading zeros off floating point values
- Compressing colors
- Transforming `none` to zero values

Fortunately, for a number of years, there have been tools available to automate this process. A popular tool, produced by Yahoo!, is called YUICompressor. YUICompressor is a Java tool based on top of the Rhino JavaScript engine. However, there is a Node port for YUICompressor called mincss. This is available as a Node module, not as command-line tool, and, therefore, can be integrated into your Node applications.

The core Grunt team has developed a Grunt task that performs similar compression. However, this does not wrap the mincss module; instead, it uses CleanCSS. CleanCSS, unlike mincss, provides a command-line interface for minifying your CSS and a Node module. The Grunt plug-in is called grunt-contrib-cssmin. Let's update our project to include this plug-in. Listing 3-36 demonstrates the updated Gruntfile.

Listing 3-36. Gruntfile with Configuration for grunt-contrib-cssmin

```
/*global module:false*/
module.exports = function(grunt) {

  // Project configuration.
  grunt.initConfig({
    // Task configuration.
    ...
    cssmin: {
      dist: {
        files: {
          'dist/css/main.css': 'css/main.css'
        }
      }
    }
  });

  // These plugins provide necessary tasks.
  grunt.loadNpmTasks('grunt-contrib-sass');
  grunt.loadNpmTasks('grunt-bower-install');
  grunt.loadNpmTasks('grunt-recess');
  grunt.loadNpmTasks('grunt-autoprefixer');
  grunt.loadNpmTasks('grunt-contrib-cssmin');

  // Default task.
  grunt.registerTask('default', [
    'sass',
    'bowerInstall',
    'recess',
    'autoprefixer',
    'cssmin'
  ]);
};
```

There should be nothing too dramatically different from our previous configurations. We've added the grunt-contrib-cssmin plug-in to be loaded and the cssmin to our default task. The configuration for cssmin itself declares a target called `dist`, which uses the `css/main.css` file (the output from our `sass` task) and outputs the compressed CSS to a new location of `dist/css/main.css`. Figure 3-5 shows the default task running for our current project. The grunt-contrib-cssmin plug-in output is last and, also helpful, reports back the size difference in the CSS before and after compression. In addition, grunt-contrib-cssmin can be configured to report the size when gzip is used in combination with minification. To optimize the delivery of your CSS, it is best to serve the content compressed, using gzip.

Gzipping of content is normally handled at the web server level, as not all clients will accept content compressed with gzip. Most modern web servers support directives to enable gzip. In the configuration for these servers, you must define by content type which files should be served. In the case of CSS, you will have to enable it for text/css. Once added, if the client requests your CSS with the Content-Encoding header set to gzip, then the web server will use gzip to compress the CSS before sending it to the client.

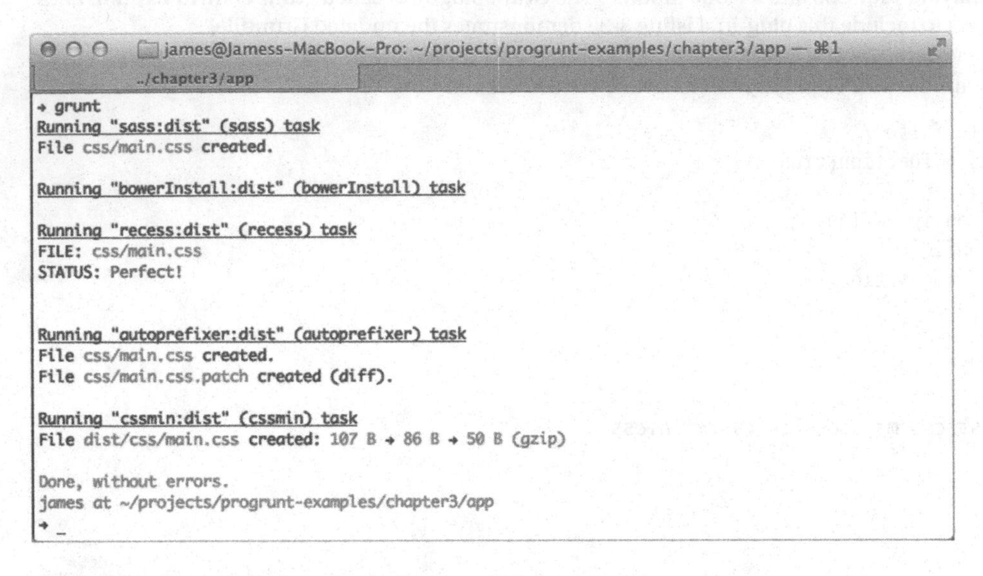

james@Jamess-MacBook-Pro: ~/projects/progrunt-examples/chapter3/app — ⌘1
../chapter3/app
→ grunt
Running "sass:dist" (sass) task
File css/main.css created.
Running "bowerInstall:dist" (bowerInstall) task
Running "recess:dist" (recess) task
FILE: css/main.css
STATUS: Perfect!
Running "autoprefixer:dist" (autoprefixer) task
File css/main.css created.
File css/main.css.patch created (diff).
Running "cssmin:dist" (cssmin) task
File dist/css/main.css created: 107 B → 86 B → 50 B (gzip)
Done, without errors.
james at ~/projects/progrunt-examples/chapter3/app
→ _

Figure 3-5. *Grunt default task running several tasks*

Before we move on to the next topic, let's look at a before and after CSS for the rules we defined earlier. For readability, whitespacing has not been stripped, but in reality, the CSS output from minification appears on a single line and, where possible, with all whitespace removed. Listing 3-37 demonstrates a CSS file that has been minified. The first modification in the outputted CSS is to the body selector's declarations. The body's color has been minified by updating the color from #333333 to #333. The second modification is the stripping of additional semicolons from the end of the border-top declaration. The next update is the comment being removed from the output. Comments can be an excellent communication tool while working on complex CSS style sheets. However, this isn't required, for when using your CSS in production, stripping comments can reduce the final size of the CSS style sheet. The paragraph selector's declaration demonstrates the minification of zero value; the padding of the paragraph is collapsed from "0px 0px" to simply "0." The floating point values have also been modified to remove the 0 that appears before the decimal point. The final modification made to the CSS is the removal of the last semicolon within each declaration block.

Removing Unused or Duplicate CSS

There is another great tool available for optimizing your CSS before releasing it. This tool is used to remove unused CSS from your style sheet and is called UnCSS. UnCSS offers a command-line tool and a Node module to be integrated to your existing application. To analyze a style sheet, UnCSS goes through the following process:

1. The HTML file is loaded by PhantomJS, a headless browser, and JavaScript is executed.
2. Used style sheets are extracted from the resulting HTML.
3. The style sheets are concatenated, and the rules are parsed, using the Node module `css-parse`.

4. Selectors that are not used within the HTML are filtered out, using `document.querySelector`.
5. The remaining rules are converted back to CSS.

Listing 3-37. Before and After CSS When Using grunt-contrib-cssmin

```
/* Before */

body {
  color: #333333;
  border-top: 2px solid #2a2a2a;;
}

/* Some comment */
p {
  margin: 0px 0px;
  padding: 0.333em 0.6em;
}

h1 {
  -webkit-transition: -webkit-transform 1s;
  transition: transform 1s;
}

/* After */

body{color:#333;border-top:2px solid #2a2a2a}

p{margin:0;padding:.333em .6em}

h1{-webkit-transition:-webkit-transform 1s;transition:transform 1s}
```

One of the limitations of UnCSS is the need for static HTML files. Obviously, not all web applications are built from a set of HTML files. There is a solution to this problem: the development of a patterns library. Patterns libraries are best described as communication tools with which a team can iterate over UI elements within an application or site. A patterns library will consist of the UI components that can be used within the application. Each component will have sample HTML and CSS. As a patterns library contains all of the HTML and CSS that will ultimately build an application, it provides a set of pages that should contain all the selectors that are defined within your CSS. If any CSS appears unused throughout these pages, it should not be required for your application. The UX team at MailChimp has produced an excellent patterns library, and it is available for viewing online at `http://ux.mailchimp.com/patterns/`.

Addy Osmani has written a Grunt plug-in that wraps UnCSS, allowing users to integrate UnCSS as part of their build process. Within the documentation for the Grunt plug-in, Addy notes the prolific use of frameworks, such as Twitter Bootstrap and TopCoat. However only 10% of these larger frameworks are actually used in most web sites. Listing 3-38 contains the configuration for grunt-uncss. The configuration of the `uncss` task is a little different from other tasks we've seen previously, as the source file type is different from the destination file. The `uncss` task takes an array of HTML files as input, and the output is a single CSS file. You may be wondering what happens if your HTML files include references to multiple CSS files. As the CSS is tokenized by UnCSS, at stage 5 in the process, all the CSS is converted back to CSS and merged in a global style sheet. Therefore, if you are using a CSS framework such as Bootstrap, all the unused CSS from

Bootstrap is removed and merged with your application code. This is the best of both worlds: you get to use a powerful CSS framework to kick-start your project while keeping your CSS for your application trim.

Let's update the application to include Bootstrap, to demonstrate the flexibility of this solution. To include Bootstrap in the project, we can use Bower. Listing 3-38 shows the command used to install Bootstrap. After installing Bootstrap, running Grunt will run our `bowerInstall` task, which automatically injects Twitter Bootstrap into the head of the HTML document. This is shown in Listing 3-39.

Listing 3-38. Gruntfile with `uncss` Task Configured

```
    ...
    cssmin: {
      dist: {
        options: {
          report: 'gzip'
        },
        files: {
          'dist/css/main.css': 'dist/css/main.css'
        }
      }
    },

    uncss: {
      dist: {
        files: {
          'dist/css/main.css': ['index.html']
        }
      }
    }
  });

  // These plugins provide necessary tasks.
  ...
  grunt.loadNpmTasks('grunt-uncss');

  // Default task.
  grunt.registerTask('default', [
    'sass',
    'bowerInstall',
    'recess',
    'autoprefixer',
    'uncss',
    'cssmin'
  ]);
};
```

Listing 3-39. Installing Twitter Bootstrap Using Bower

```
bower install  bootstrap --save-dev
```

Now that Bootstrap has been installed in our application, if you rerun the `grunt` task, you should note a shift in the size of our CSS. Previously, our CSS was a few bytes. Now the starting size of our CSS has jumped to approximately 120KB. After UnCSS runs over our CSS, the size is considerably reduced from 120KB to 2.39KB.

The CSS output in `dist/css/main.css` contains the CSS from Bootstrap and our application CSS combined in a single file. This is another great performance win, as we should strive to reduce the number of CSS files within our page, as, typically, fewer requests per page are better. Fewer requests typically improve performance, due to latency costs, while establishing new connections. This is particularly prevalent for devices accessing sites on slower network connections. For a more in-depth study and explanation of browser performance, I recommend reading *Higher Performance Browser Networking* by Ilya Grigorik (O'Reilly Media, 2013).

As you can see from Listing 3-40, our `index.html` file is still currently referencing our unoptimized version of the CSS file. Ideally, before shipping our application to the public, we'd want to update the references to the optimized CSS files. Fortunately, Grunt can also help with this task as well. Let's see how.

Listing 3-40. HTML Head Section Updated Automatically with Bootstrap Injected

```
<head>
<meta charset="utf-8">
<meta http-equiv="X-UA-Compatible" content="IE=edge">
<title>Pro Grunt.js: Todo List</title>
<meta name="description" content="">
<meta name="viewport" content="width=device-width, initial-scale=1">

<!-- bower:css -->
<link rel="stylesheet" href="build/bower_components/bootstrap/dist/css/bootstrap.css" />
<!-- endbower -->
<link rel="stylesheet" href="css/main.css">
</head>
```

Packaging Your App for Production

As noted in the previous section, we now have an optimized CSS file, but it is not currently being used within our project. As Grunt works on the principle of multiple tasks working together on a set of files, each task modifying the files and producing an output for the next task to pick up, we have to introduce a task to update our HTML with references to optimized CSS, in much the same way as our `bowerInstall` task injects references to Bower components installed for our project.

The Yeoman team has created a plug-in that solves this problem, and it is called grunt-usemin. This plug-in is a little different from the ones encountered thus far. It introduces two tasks: `useminPrepare` and `usemin`.

The `useminPrepare` task should be used to ready your files for the `usemin` task to update your HTML file with the correct references to the static assets, such as CSS. Grunt-usemin, like grunt-bower-install, uses special HTML comments within the HTML to cleverly replace references to the files. The grunt-usemin plug-in also introduces a little magic to our project, as it auto-generates configuration for our tasks, such as concatenation and minification. Therefore, we can remove the `cssmin` configuration from our Gruntfile, as `usemin` will auto-generate it for us.

Listing 3-41 illustrates the modifications needed by the HTML to support `usemin`, in particular the blocks added to support rewriting of asset names.

Listing 3-41. Modified index.html with Additional Blocks for usemin

```
<head>
<meta charset="utf-8">
<meta http-equiv="X-UA-Compatible" content="IE=edge">
<title>Pro Grunt.js: Todo List</title>
<meta name="description" content="">
<meta name="viewport" content="width=device-width, initial-scale=1">

<!-- build:css css/main.css -->
<!-- bower:css -->
<link rel="stylesheet" href="build/bower_components/bootstrap/dist/css/bootstrap.css" />
<!-- endbower -->
<link rel="stylesheet" href="css/main.css">
<!-- endbuild -->
</head>
```

Now that we have prepared our HTML file for use with usemin, we have to configure the useminPrepare and usemin tasks within our Gruntfile. Listing 3-42 demonstrates the output from the usemin task, most notably the rewritten path to support the new optimized CSS.

Listing 3-42. Gruntfile with useminPrepare and usemin Added

```
  copy: {
    dist: {
      expand: true,
      cwd: 'app/',
      src: 'index.html',
      dest: 'dist/'
    }
  },

  useminPrepare: {
    dist: {
      src: 'app/index.html',
      dest: 'dist/'
    }
  },

  usemin: {
    html: 'dist/index.html'
  }

  // Default task.
grunt.registerTask('default', [
  'useminPrepare',
  'sass',
  'bowerInstall',
  'autoprefixer',
  'recess',
  'uncss',
  'usemin'
]);
```

As you can see, the actual configuration for useminPrepare and usemin themselves is rather trim. We inform usemin where the HTML file exists for our preparation and then one to be used by usemin. At the moment, we do not have an index.html file in our dist folder; therefore, we have to introduce a new Grunt plug-in called grunt-contrib-copy. This plug-in is used to copy files or folders from one place to another within a project. In our project, we will use grunt-contrib-copy to copy the index.html file from app/index.html to dist/index.html. This file will then be processed by usemin to update the references to the optimized CSS. Having an index.html file in our dist folder allows us to work locally with a development copy of our application before building a version for releasing that contains the correct references to the optimized CSS. Listing 3-43 contains the configuration for grunt-contrib-copy.

Listing 3-43. Head Element Has Been Modified to Contain Reference to Optimized CSS

```
<head>
<meta charset="utf-8">
<meta http-equiv="X-UA-Compatible" content="IE=edge">
<title>Pro Grunt.js: Todo List</title>
<meta name="description" content="">
<meta name="viewport" content="width=device-width, initial-scale=1">
<link rel="stylesheet" href="css/main.css">
</head>
```

As you can see, the index.html now contains a reference to the optimized CSS, ready for deployment to production. In the following section, we will look at asset versioning of optimized caching of static assets and how Grunt can help us with this process.

Versioning

In the final section of this chapter, we'll see how we can use Grunt to further improve the performance of our production code. In this section, we'll look at how we can ship versioned assets. The primary reason to ship versioned assets is to safely set far future cache headers for our static assets. Setting far future headers improves performance, as clients can cache a copy of your assets, preventing them from having to return to your server to re-request the asset on each page load. Typically, we will set a far future expires header on assets such as CSS, web fonts, and JavaScript. For an example of web server configuration for expires headers, check out HTML5 Boilerplate's .htaccess file. This provides a great starting point for people using the Apache web server and sets the majority of static assets to expire a month from the time they were accessed.

As mentioned, Grunt can help with the delivery of static assets with far future headers. Simply sending an expires header with a far future date can be dangerous. Any updates to that asset will not be picked up until the cache expires and the client re-requests the asset from the server. There are a couple solutions to this problem. One popular approach is to add a cache buster to the URL for the asset. When the asset itself changes, the cache buster is updated, forcing the client to re-request the asset from the server. Listing 3-44 shows a dummy URL for a CSS file with a cache buster appended.

Listing 3-44. Dummy CSS URL with Cache Buster Appended

```
http://mysite.com/styles/app.css?c=20140303
```

Unfortunately, some proxy servers are configured by default not to cache URLs that contain query strings. Therefore, we need an alternatively approach. Listing 3-45 shows both approaches.

Listing 3-45. Alternative Asset Version Approaches

```
http://mysite.com/0.1.0/styles/app.css
http://mysite.com/styles/app.0.1.0.css
```

In the first approach, the version number is inserted into the path to the assets. This is the approach the BBC currently takes to version its assets. For example, the BBC homepage has the following reference: `http://static.bbci.co.uk/h4clock/0.69.3/style/h4clock.css`. In this case, the version is 0.69.3. The alternative approach, including the version in the asset file name, is used by jQuery when serving jQuery from its CDN. For example, the URL for the latest version of jQuery, at the time of writing, is `http://code.jquery.com/jquery-1.11.0.min.js`.

There is a Grunt plug-in, grunt-rev, available to perform version asset production. The grunt-rev plug-in generates a hash based on the contents of your file. It offers a number of algorithms for generating the hash, such as md5 and sha256. The hash generated for a file is injected before the file extension. In addition to this, grunt-rev works perfectly with the usemin plug-in introduced in the previous section. Listing 3-46 shows the latest configuration for both of these files.

Listing 3-46. Configuration for Static Asset Versioning

```
rev: {
  dist: {
    src: 'dist/css/main.css'
  }
}
```

As you can see, the CSS generated in the temporary folder as part of the earlier tasks is now picked up by the `rev` task and dropped into the `dist/css` folder. Once this has completed, `usemin` modifies the `index.html` file in the `dist` folder with the path to the newly versioned CSS. The benefit of using hashes over timestamps, in this case, is that the hash should only change when the contents of the file itself changes. This is particularly important if you have multiple teams generating the same static assets. You only want the asset name to change when there has been a genuine change to the contents of the file.

Summary

In this chapter, we've explored how to use Grunt to ease our development workflow when working with HTML and CSS. We started with a brief introduction into CSS preprocessors and how Grunt can aid us with compiling our CSS. After this, we moved on to Bower, a powerful front-end dependency manager, which can be integrated with Grunt to make managing front-end libraries within our projects easy. The remainder of the chapter looked at a number of plug-ins that can be used to help optimize our HTML and CSS before releasing it onto the public Web.

In the next chapter, we'll continue to look at how Grunt can help when working with front-end technology, as you discover a powerful set of plug-ins to help with JavaScript development.

CHAPTER 4

Using Grunt with JavaScript

At this point, I've covered setting up Grunt on a project, and you've seen how it can help when working with CSS and HTML. Next, we'll start to explore the benefits of using Grunt while developing in JavaScript. As mentioned, when you were first introduced to Grunt, it is written on top of the Node.js platform, a JavaScript engine. This fact makes Grunt the perfect tool to use while working with JavaScript, as developers can exploit existing Node.js modules to rapidly process plug-ins to extend their workflow. In this chapter, I'll cover how Grunt can help with JavaScript templating, working with JavaScript modules, and automated testing. First, I'll outline how we plan to extend our to-do list application and use Grunt to automate our workflow and build process.

Enhancing Our To-Do List Application

At present, our to-do list application is still very basic. We've got an outline of HTML and CSS that is all built using Grunt. In the course of this chapter, we will continue to build on this application, by using Grunt to add a rich user interface powered by the popular JavaScript framework BackBone.js. In addition, we'll look at how we can test our application, produce documentation, and build our application for production by linting and minifying the JavaScript.

To get started, let's install Backbone.js using Bower. Figure 4-1 demonstrates the installation of Backbone with Bower.

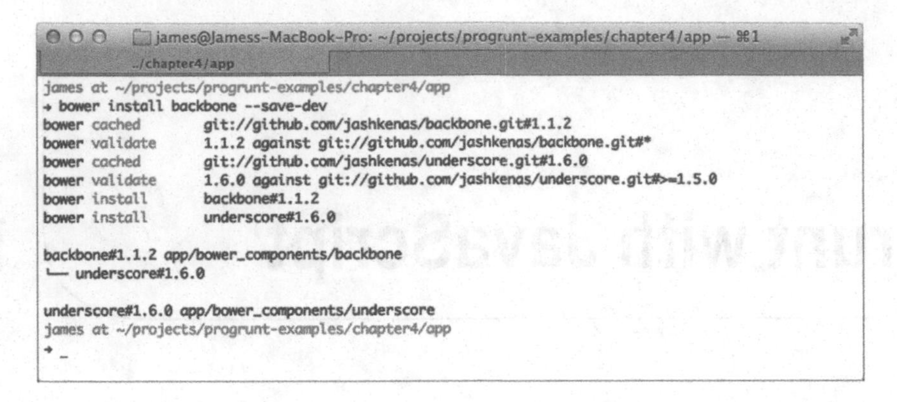

james@Jamess-MacBook-Pro: ~/projects/progrunt-examples/chapter4/app — ⌘1
../chapter4/app
james at ~/projects/progrunt-examples/chapter4/app
→ bower install backbone --save-dev
bower cached git://github.com/jashkenas/backbone.git#1.1.2
bower validate 1.1.2 against git://github.com/jashkenas/backbone.git#*
bower cached git://github.com/jashkenas/underscore.git#1.6.0
bower validate 1.6.0 against git://github.com/jashkenas/underscore.git#>=1.5.0
bower install backbone#1.1.2
bower install underscore#1.6.0
backbone#1.1.2 app/bower_components/backbone
└── underscore#1.6.0
underscore#1.6.0 app/bower_components/underscore
james at ~/projects/progrunt-examples/chapter4/app

Figure 4-1. *Installing Backbone.js also leads to underscore.js being installed, as Backbone depends on this library*

Next, we have to update our application. Running Grunt will update the `index.html` file in the root of our application to include references to Backbone.js and underscore.js.

Backbone.js provides an MV* architecture allowing developers to separate application logic into logical parts. It loosely follows the same pattern that many modern web application frameworks, such as Ruby on Rails, follow. This will allow us to develop our to-do application in modules: one responsible for storing data, another for presenting our data, and yet another for controlling the application flow. This leads us nicely to the topic of how Grunt.js can help us develop our JavaScript applications, using modules and optimizing them for delivery in production.

JavaScript Modules

The benefits of developing applications with distinct modules are well understood. Modular software often leads to improved maintainability, as each module is designed to perform a single task and can be decoupled from other parts of the system. In addition, modules help encapsulate functionality, hiding the implementation details from users of the module. This makes it easier to modify the internals of a module without affecting other parts of the system.

Most modern programming languages have native support for distributing and importing modules, but, unfortunately, the current iteration of JavaScript does not. However, ECMAScript 6, also known as Harmony or ES6, the next version of JavaScript, will offer support for importing modules into our JavaScript applications. While browsers, at the time of writing, do not offer support for ES6 module loading, we can still use frameworks and tools to start using modules within our JavaScript application today.

Aside from the ES6 definition of a modular format, there are two other popular formats currently used, known as AMD and CommonJS. Before looking at how Grunt.js can help us utilize the power of modules within our JavaScript applications, let's take a brief look at each of these formats.

AMD

AMD stands for *Asynchronous Module Definition* and aims to allow JavaScript developers to use modules within browsers today. AMD arises from real-world experiences of the Dojo framework with the use of XHR + eval and seeks to avoid the weaknesses in these. The AMD format states how to define modules and the dependencies to be loaded asynchronously.

AMD offers a number of benefits over the traditional method, including JavaScript within a web page. Instead of multiple script tags and a pollulated global namespace, there is a single JavaScript application file, and all other modules are loaded asynchronously. Each module encapsulates its own functionality and has to explicitly return an interface for other modules to utilize.

There are two fundamental concepts used when defining and using AMD modules. The first of these is the function `define`. The `define` function provides a method for naming a module, declaring the dependencies and the implementation of the module. Listing 4-1 illustrates a very basic AMD module that returns two properties: keys and cities. Listing 4-1 demonstrates some fundmental aspects of the AMD modules. The `define` function is used to define our module, and it accepts three parameters: the module name, the module dependencies, and the callback function containing the module's implementation. In this example, we've named our module `simpleModule` and defined a single dependency on the framework `underscore`. The final parameter is the implementation. It is important to note that `underscore` is passed into our callback as a parameter, so that it can be used within our module. By allowing dependencies to be passed into the scope of our module, the need for modules to be assigned to the global namespace is removed. This reduces the risk of side effects across modules, as each module only accesses variables within its scope.

Listing 4-1. A Basic AMD Module

```
define(
  'simpleModule',
  ['/underscore'],
  function(_) {

    var places = {
      'nyc': 'New York',
      'lon': 'London'
    };

    return {
        keys: _.keys(places),
        cities: _.values(places).sort()
    };
});
```

In Listing 4-1, an object is returned with two values attached: keys and cities. However, AMD does not prescribe the type returned by a module. For example, it is acceptable for a module to return a single value or a function that can be executed later. Before concluding our introduction to defining AMD modules, it is important to note that it is best pratice not to name modules, and each AMD module should be defined in its own file. By applying these two principles, the portability of modules improves, and other developers can move modules into different paths to give the module a different name/ID.

Now that we have a module defined, we need a way of including it within our application, so that it can be used. Another fundamental concept of AMD modules is the `require` function. The `require` function is used to load modules. Listing 4-2 demonstrates a small JavaScript application that loads and uses the module defined in Listing 4-1.

Listing 4-2. Using `require` to Load and Use Other Modules

```
define(['jquery'], function($) {
  require(['data/cities'], function(data) {
    $('#cities').text(data.cities.join(', '));
  });
});
```

In Listing 4-2, we see the use of the `require` function for the first time. In this particular example, we're using `require` within the scope of a new module. The module has a dependency on jQuery and then uses the `require` function to load the module we defined in Listing 4-1. As of yet, we haven't explored the topic of module IDs. In Listing 4-2, we load our module (defined in Listing 4-1) with the module ID of `data/cities`. Module IDs can be considered the equivalent of folder paths. To help illustrate this, Figure 4-2 shows a folder structure that represents the example from Listing 4-2.

Figure 4-2. *Examples from Listings 4-1 and 4-2 demonstrate module ID*

In the example from Listing 4-2, we use the module ID of `data/cities`, which matches the folder structure highlighted in Figure 4-2. The `data` part of the module ID represents the folder, while the `cities` part represents the file `cities.js`.

Thus far, I've discussed the core concepts regarding AMD modules, but I have yet to discuss module loading in practice. There are two popular JavaScript frameworks that implement AMD module loading: `require.js` and `curl.js`. For the remainder of the book, we'll be using `require.js` to load AMD modules. Bower can be used to add `require.js` to the project, as demonstrated in Figure 4-3.

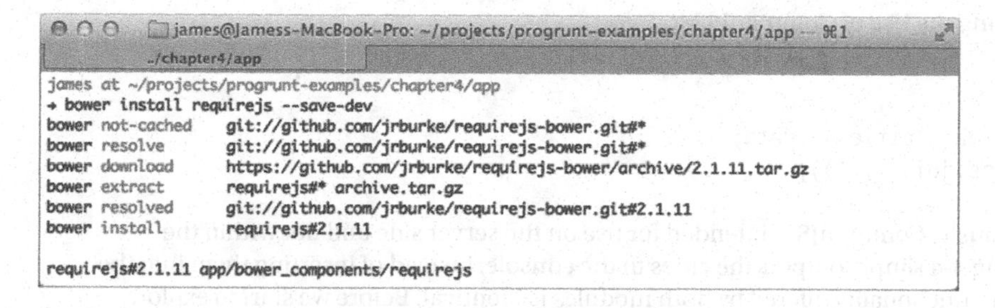

Figure 4-3. *Using Bower to add* `require.js` *to a project*

After running `grunt` on the project, `require.js` should now be loaded into our sample application. Before looking at how we can fully integrate `require.js` into our project, let's explore an alternative JavaScript modular format, CommonJS.

CommonJS

CommonJS is an alternative JavaScript modular format and aims to standardize both modules and packages by specifying a simple API for declaring service-side modules. The CommonJS specification is not concerned with broader issues of io and file systems. CommonJS was already discussed in Chapter 2, when Node.js modules were first introduced. The structure of CommonJS modules is simplier than AMD modules, as there is no wrapper function. Instead, functionality is made available to dependent code via an `exports` variable. To use a module, there is a `require` function available; however, as modules are not loaded asynchronously, they are returned immediately. Listing 4-3 demonstrates the CommonJS implementation of the module from Listing 4-1.

Listing 4-3. CommonJS Implementation of Simple Places Module

```
var _ = require('underscore');

var places = {
  "nyc": "New York",
  "lon": "London"
};

exports.data = {
  keys: _.keys(places),
  cities: _.values(places).sort()
};
```

The module in Listing 4-3 offers the same functionality as the one defined in Listing 4-1. The key difference in this implementation is how we define dependencies and expose the module functionality. Dependencies are loaded with the use of the `require` function, and functionality is exposed using the `exports` variable that is injected into our module when it is included in an application. Listing 4-4 demonstrates the use of our very simple CommonJS module.

Listing 4-4. Demonstrating the Use of CommonJS Modules

```
'use strict';

var data = require('./data/cities').data;
console.log(data.cities.join(', '));
```

As mentioned previously, CommonJS is intended for use on the server side and not within the browser. Therefore, Listing 4-4 simply outputs the cities to the console, instead of inserting them into the page. However, the actual functionality offered by both modules is identical. Before we start to explore using AMD modules in our Grunt.js workflow, it is important to note that there is a new universal module loader—known as Browserify—available. Browserify allows you to develop CommonJS modules and then bundle them into a single JavaScript file to load into the browser. This offers the additional benefits of being able to use the same JavaScript on the server and the client side without modification. Browserify has also conceived transformers that allow CommonJS and AMD modules to be loaded into the same application. Although it would be good practice to develop your application with a mixture of module formats, this can come in handy if your favorite front-end JavaScript framework is only published as an AMD module.

Combining Grunt.js and JavaScript Modules

Let's now modify our application to use `require.js` to load JavaScript modules while we are developing our application. This allows us to develop our application in a modular functionality, encouraging us not to mix responsibilities between modules and essentially leading to a more decoupled set of modules. As illustrated in Listing 4-5, we have jQuery, Bootstrap, Underscore.js, Backbone.js, and `require.js` included in our application.

Listing 4-5. JavaScript Includes Currently in Our Application

```
<!-- build:js js/app.js -->
<!-- bower:js -->
<script src="bower_components/jquery/dist/jquery.js"></script>
<script src="bower_components/bootstrap/dist/js/bootstrap.js"></script>
<script src="bower_components/underscore/underscore.js"></script>
<script src="bower_components/backbone/backbone.js"></script>
<script src="bower_components/requirejs/require.js"></script>
<!-- endbower -->
<script src="js/main.js"></script>
<!-- endbuild -->
```

Although this works effectively in development, when we later look to compile our JavaScript into a single file for release, we may encounter some issues, as the goal libraries may clash with the ones used by require.js. To resolve this issue, the JavaScript include can be modified to use a new Grunt plug-in called grunt-bower-requirejs. The grunt-bower-requirejs plug-in is similar to grunt-bower-install and will read your bower components and merge them with your `require.js` path configuration. Listing 4-6 demostrates a modified `index.html` file containing the configuration required to use the grunt-bower-install plug-in.

Listing 4-6. `index.html` Modified to Support require.js

```
<!-- build:js js/main.js -->
  <script src="bower_components/requirejs/require.js"></script>
  <script src="js/paths.js"></script>
  <script src="js/main.js"></script>
<!-- endbuild -->
```

In Listing 4-6, `index.html` has been modified to remove the grunt-bower-install configuration. In its place, three script tags have been introduced. The first includes the `require.js` library itself; the second is a JavaScript file containing `require.js` path configuration; and the final script tag loads our application. The `path.js` file is used by the grunt-bower-requirejs plug-in to merge our `bower` components. Listing 4-7 demonstrates the `path.js` file before grunt-bower-requirejs is run. To begin, the file simply needs a call to the `require.js` configuration method with an empty configuration object.

Listing 4-7. `path.js` File Before grunt-bower-requirejs

```
requirejs.config({});
```

Next, our Gruntfile.js must be modified to support the new grunt-bower-requirejs plug-in. Listing 4-8 demonstrates the configuration added to our Gruntfile.js to support the new plug-in.

Listing 4-8. Configuration for grunt-bower-requirejs to Maintain require.js Paths with bower Components

```
bower: {
    dist: {
      rjsConfig: 'app/js/paths.js',
      options: {
        baseUrl: 'app/'
      }
    }
}
```

The first option defines the path to our `require.js` configuration. This will be the file that the task will modify when run. The second option, `baseUrl`, defines the URL that is prepended to all paths. This is useful when you want to move your modules to a new location within the same project, for example, when building your application for production. Running the `bower` task should now modify `path.js` to match Listing 4-9. This will allow us to use `bower` components within our AMD modules.

Listing 4-9. `path.js` After grunt-bower-requirejs Has Been Configured and Run

```
requirejs.config({
  paths: {
    backbone: "bower_components/backbone/backbone",
    bootstrap: "bower_components/bootstrap/dist/js/bootstrap",
    jquery: "bower_components/jquery/dist/jquery",
    requirejs: "bower_components/requirejs/require",
    underscore: "bower_components/underscore/underscore"
  },
  packages: [

  ]
});
```

The third script included in the `index.html` file will be our main application JavaScript module. This will be the starting point of our application that will be used to load other modules and initialize our application. Listing 4-10 illustrates the `main.js` file.

Listing 4-10. `main.js` File Containing Our Initilize Code

```
require(['js/app'], function(app) {
  $(function() {
    app.init();
  });
});
```

Listing 4-10 uses `require` to load the module known as `js/app`. Once loaded, jQuery isReady shorthand is used, then the `js/app` module is expected to return an `init` function. Listing 4-11 defines the module `js/app`, our first AMD module.

Listing 4-11. Application Module Used As the Starting Point of Our Application Code

```
define(function() {

  var initialize = function() {
    console.log('app.init');
  };

  return {
    init: initialize
  };
});
```

Listing 4-11 defines a simple AMD module that currently does not depend on any other modules. It defines a private method called `initialize` and exposes this to users of the module, via the return statement, as an `init` function. If you now load the application in your favorite browser, you should see “app.init” printed to the console, as shown in Figure 4-4.

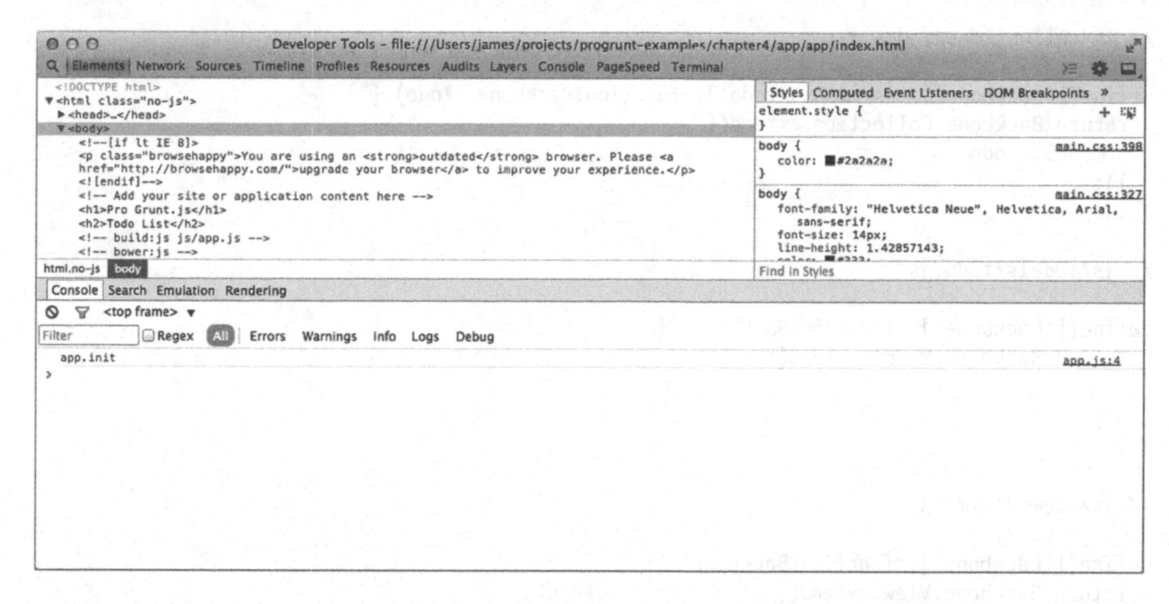

Figure 4-4. Demonstration of application module being loaded using require.js

Now that we have confirmed that our application is loading AMD modules, let's add some more skeleton code for our to-do application. Listing 4-12 lists several new modules that will make up the total to-do application.

Listing 4-12. AMD Modules to Make Up the Complete Application

```
// js/app.js

define([
  'js/collections/todos',
  'js/views/form',
  'js/views/todo-item'
  ], function(Collection, FormView, TodoView) {

  var initialize = function() {
    console.log('app.init');
    var todos = new Collection();
    new FormView().render();
    new TodoView(todos).render();
  };

  return {
    init: initialize
  };
});
```

```
// js/collections/todos.js

define(['backbone', 'js/models/todo'], function(Backbone, Todo) {
  return Backbone.Collection.extend({
    model: Todo
  });
});

// js/models/todo.js

define(['backbone'], function(Backbone) {
  return Backbone.Model.extend({

  });
});

// js/views/form.js

define(['backbone'], function(Backbone) {
  return Backbone.View.extend({

    tagName: 'div',

    className: 'todo-form',

    render: function() {

    }
  });
});

// js/views/todo-item.js

define(['backbone'], function(Backbone) {
  return Backbone.View.extend({

    tagName: 'li',

    className: 'todo-item',

    render: function() {

    }
  });
});
```

Listing 4-12 adds four new AMD modules: a Backbone collection, model, and two views. At the moment, the application does not do a lot, as we have not defined templates for the Backbone views to render. However, it does set up the application structure with which we can start to improve our workflow. In the current state, to add a new module to our application is relatively easy: we create a new file and then add a reference to it. However, we do not have a process for optimizing our JavaScript code in production. Let's update our Gruntfile to optimize the JavaScript that appears in the `dist` folder.

First, let's introduce a new Grunt.js plug-in to compile our `require.js` modules into a single file. As discussed in the previous chapter, in production, you want to aim for the fewest number of HTTP calls, which means fewer assets. In our particular example, if we are able to combine our JavaScript files in production, we will reduce the number of connections from 11 to 1. The Grunt.js plug-in we will use is called grunt-contrib-requirejs. The plug-in grunt-contrib-plugin can be used to automate the running of the `require.js` optimizer. The require.js optimizer is designed to parse a JavaScript application that is using AMD modules and combine the modules into a single file. In addition to this, the optimizer can also minify the combined JavaScript, using the library known as Uglify. Listing 4-13 demonstrates the configuration for grunt-contrib-requirejs.

Listing 4-13. Adding grunt-contrib-requirejs Configuration

```
requirejs: {
  dist: {
    options: {
      baseUrl: 'app/',
      name: '../.tmp/concat/js/main',
      out: 'dist/js/main.js',
      optimize: 'uglify2',
      paths: {
        backbone: 'bower_components/backbone/backbone',
        bootstrap: 'bower_components/bootstrap/dist/js/bootstrap',
        jquery: 'bower_components/jquery/dist/jquery',
        requirejs: 'bower_components/requirejs/require',
        underscore: 'bower_components/underscore/underscore',
        handlebars: 'bower_components/handlebars/handlebars'
      }
    }
  }
},
```

The new configuration has a number of options set. First, the `baseUrl` is set to match that of the application path, as our application resides within the app folder. This leads to the AMD modules being correctly located by the require.js optimizer. The next configuration option, `main`, indicates to the optimizer the main file that is the starting point of the application. This points to the `.tmp` directly, as we want to combine our AMD modules with the concentrated JavaScript produced as part of the usemin plug-in. Therefore, the `requirejs` task will have to run after the `concat` task has completed. The `out` option, as you might expect, dictates where the output from the task should be placed. Finally, the task provides the ability to specify which optimization should be applied. In our configuration, we've opted for UglifyJS2. To disable optimization, the value of `none` can be passed.

Once this has been added to your Gruntfile.js file, you will have to add the task to the default task. Listing 4-14 shows the updated default task.

Listing 4-14. Default Task Modified to Include grunt-contrib-requirejs

```
grunt.loadNpmTasks('grunt-contrib-requirejs');

// Default task.
grunt.registerTask('default', [
  'useminPrepare',
  'sass',
  'bowerInstall',
```

```
  'autoprefixer',
  'recess',
  'uncss',
  'copy',
  'cssmin',
  'concat',
  'requirejs',
  'rev',
  'usemin'
]);
```

It is important to note the order of tasks. We must include the `requirejs` task after `concat`, to ensure that our application file has been concatentated into the `.tmp` folder before the `requirejs` task is run. Now that the new task is loaded and the `requirejs` task has been added to the default task, running grunt should produce a `js/main.js` file.

Before moving on to the next topic, we have to further optimize the JavaScript output to the `dist` folder. We must modify the `grunt-rev` task to include our JavaScript file as well. This is a minor modification to ensure that the `dist` target matches the one in Listing 4-15.

Listing 4-15. Updating grunt-rev to Include JavaScript, to Ensure Caching Is Effective

```
rev: {
  dist: {
    src: ['dist/css/main.css', 'dist/js/main.js']
  }
},
```

Cleaning the Build Process

As the build process increases, it is likely that you may have artifacts that remain built as part of the build. A common example is a temporary file before it has been minified but after it has been generated as part of a concentration process. These files are generally harmless, as they typically do not appear in the production code. However, it is best practice to ensure that each build is clean. A task can be introduced to solve this problem, and the one we will add is `grunt-contrib-clean`. The grunt-contrib-clean plug-in can be used to remove particular files or recursively clean a directory. Listing 4-16 illustrates the configuration used for the to-do application.

Listing 4-16. Configuraton for grunt-contrib-clean

```
clean: {
  tmp: {
    src: ['.tmp', '.sass-cache', 'dist', 'app/js/template.js']
  }
}
```

The configuration outlined in Listing 4-16 will simply remove the `.tmp`, `.sass-cache`, and `dist` folders. All three of these folders are generated as part of the build process, so there is no harm in removing them. It is a good idea to add the `clean` task to the default task (see Listing 4-17), so that the application is cleaned each time `grunt` is run. Best practice suggests that it should be the first task run, to ensure that each build is in a pristine state before being run. If `clean` is added only to the end of the build process, there is a possibility that a previous build that failed will populate newer builds.

Listing 4-17. Illustration of a Modified Default Task

```
// Default task.
grunt.registerTask('default', [
  'clean',
  'useminPrepare',
  'sass',
  'bowerInstall',
  'autoprefixer',
  'recess',
  ....
]);
```

JavaScript Templating

With our AMD modules integrated as part of workflow, let's turn our attention to the implementation of the to-do application. In this section, we will explore the use of JavaScript templating libraries and the use of Grunt to automate the generation of these templates into our workflow.

With modern web applications with rich user interfaces, it is important to separate the application into modules that perform specific tasks, as outlined in the previous section. This has lead to the rapid emergence of front-end frameworks that follow the common design pattern of model-view-controller, alternatively known as MVC.

In the MVC design pattern, application modules are divided into three concerns. The model contains the state of the application; the view is the representation of that state; and the controller orchestrates actions fired from the view to modify the state in the model and notify the view of changes to the state. In most modern frameworks, the views are generated by using a templating engine. Often, frameworks, such as Backbone, do not prescribe the templating engine to be used and allow the developer to choose the engine that best suits his/her needs.

There is a vast set of templating engines available for JavaScript, offering powerful features such as partials and helpers. The capabilities of each engine vary from the simplest form, such as the underscore.js `template` function, to more feature-rich functions such as handlebars.js. For the majority of our examples, we will be using handlebars.js, and we will integrate this into the Grunt.js workflow for the to-do application. Before updating the Grunt workflow, let's explore the various implementation strageties that can be applied when using JavaScript templating.

The first technique, and the simplest of the three, is to not use a template engine but to build the view programmatically. Listing 4-18 demonstrates building a Backbone view, using jQuery to create an `h1` element and assigning a local variable as the text. In this trivial example, the solution may appear adequate, but this approach quickly starts to break down when the views become more complex and we have to iterate over a number of items.

Listing 4-18. Simple View Rendering with Backbone.js

```
define(['backbone'], function(Backbone) {
  return Backbone.View.extend({

    tagName: 'div',

    className: 'todo-form',

    render: function() {
      var title = "Hello World!";
```

```
      this.$el.html(
        $('<h1 />').text(title)
      );
    }
  });
});
```

The next approach is to use inline templates in which the template string is stored within a local variable and passed to the template engine. In Listing 4-19, the underscore.js `template` function has been used to demonstrate the use of inline templates.

Listing 4-19. Using Inline Templates with the `template` Function from underscore.js

```
define(['backbone'], function(Backbone) {
  return Backbone.View.extend({

    tagName: 'div',

    className: 'todo-form',

    template: _.template('<h1><%= title %></h1>'),

    render: function() {
      var title = "Hello World!";
      this.$el.html(
        this.template({title: title})
      );
    }
  });
});
```

This approach suffers from the same issues as the first approach: an inline template works well when the template is simple. If we were to expand the sample in Listing 4-19 to be used as a multiple-line template with an iterative loop, this would quickly become unmaintainable.

The third approach solves the issues associated with the first two approaches by improving the maintainability. The templates are stored within script tags within the DOM. Each template is given a unique ID, so that it can be selected from the DOM, and its contents then passed to the template engine. Listing 4-20 demonstrates loading a template from the DOM and passing it to the underscore.js `template` function.

Listing 4-20. Loading Template from the DOM

```
// index.html

<script type="text/template" id="title-tmpl">
  <h1><%= title %></h1>
</script>

// view.js

define(['backbone', 'underscore'], function(Backbone, _) {
  return Backbone.View.extend({
```

```
    tagName: 'div',

    className: 'todo-form',

    template: _.template(document.getElementById('title-tmpl').innerHTML),

    render: function() {
      var title = "Hello World!";
      this.$el.html(
        this.template({title: title})
      );
    }
  });
});
```

The key difference between this solution and the first two is the method used to load the template content. Instead of storing the template within the JavaScript application code, the template has been shifted to the DOM. The template content is loaded by using `document.getElementById` to pass the template content to the `template` function. This resolves the issue of maintaining more complex templates, as the templates are far more readable, because the tags can be edited as any other HTML template. However, this approach does introduce the issue of your page being bloated with additional script tags, one for each template. This may not be an issue if you have a few templates, but it can quickly escalate and introduce a new maintainability concern. This leads nicely to our final solution, which uses Grunt to improve maintainability and readability of our JavaScript templates.

In this final approach, we will use a Grunt plug-in to pre-compile the templates into a single JavaScript template (`JST`) file. It is important to note that in this solution, we will switch from the underscore.js template to handlebars.js. Before we can start writing templates, however, we must add a new plug-in to the Grunt.js file. The plug-in that will be using in this solution is grunt-contrib-handlebars. Listing 4-21 shows the configuration that will be used to generate the `JST` file.

Listing 4-21. Grunt Configuration for grunt-contrib-handlebars

```
handlebars: {
    dist: {
      options: {
        namespace: 'JST',
        amd: true
      },
      files: {
        'app/js/template.js': ['build/templates/**/*.hbs']
      }
    }
  },
```

The preceding configuration will load all templates from the `build/templates` folder and compile them into a single AMD module that is output to `app/js/template.js`. This will then allow the templates to be used within our AMD modules, by adding the template module as a dependency. Listing 4-22 demonstrates the view, updated to use the new template module.

Listing 4-22. Using the Template Module Within the View Module

```
define(['backbone', 'js/template'], function(Backbone, Template) {
  return Backbone.View.extend({

    tagName: 'div',

    className: 'todo-form',

    template: Template["build/templates/form.hbs"],

    render: function() {
      var title = "Hello World!";
      this.$el.html(
        this.template({title: title})
      );
    }
  });
});
```

The primary difference between Listings 4-20 and 4-22 is removal of the template from HTML. This brings two benefits, the first being that we reduce the problem of managing which templates to include within the HTML. This is a problem for complex applications that have many templates and many pages for which templates are needed for every page. Removing the templates from the HTML also reduces the payload of the initial page load, which is great for load-time performance. The templates are compiled into the JavaScript application code and compressed in production, which further improves performance. The second benefit is the separation that occurs by having each individual template in a separate file. This leads to easier maintainence, as you can focus on a particular template without worrying about affecting other templates. Listing 4-23 shows a sample template.

Listing 4-23. Sample Template Saved in `build/templates/form.hbs`

```
<h1>{{title}}</h1>
```

To use handlebars in the project, we also must add it, using `bower`. Once added, the non-AMD version of the handlebars library is included by grunt-bower-requirejs. Therefore, we have to add a shim in order for require.js to export it as a global. Listing 4-24 demonstrates the shim being added to the `paths.js` and `Gruntfile.js`.

Listing 4-24. Modified Configuration for handlebar.js

```
// paths.js
requirejs.config({
  shim: {
    handlebars: {
      exports: 'Handlebars'
    }
  },
  paths: {
    backbone: 'bower_components/backbone/backbone',
    bootstrap: 'bower_components/bootstrap/dist/js/bootstrap',
    jquery: 'bower_components/jquery/dist/jquery',
```

```
    requirejs: 'bower_components/requirejs/require',
    underscore: 'bower_components/underscore/underscore',
    handlebars: 'bower_components/handlebars/handlebars'
  },
  packages: [

  ]
});

// Gruntfile.js

  requirejs: {
      dist: {
        options: {
          baseUrl: 'app',
          name: '../.tmp/concat/js/main',
          out: 'dist/js/main.js',
          optimize: 'uglify2',
          mainConfig: 'app/js/paths.js',
          shim: {
            handlebars: {
              exports: 'Handlebars'
            }
          },
          paths: {
            backbone: 'bower_components/backbone/backbone',
            bootstrap: 'bower_components/bootstrap/dist/js/bootstrap',
            jquery: 'bower_components/jquery/dist/jquery',
            requirejs: 'bower_components/requirejs/require',
            underscore: 'bower_components/underscore/underscore',
            handlebars: 'bower_components/handlebars/handlebars'
          }
        }
      }
    },
```

This concludes the section on JavaScript templating. You have seen how to create, compile, and optimize templating for production. I covered the use of handlebars.js; however, there are many other templating options available. Another popular templating engine is Jade, often used with the Express framework.

JavaScript Linting

In the previous chapter, I discussed the use of RECESS, a CSS lint tool from Twitter, to ensure that the CSS in our projects conform to a set of styling rules and to detect common errors. In this section, we will explore the use of JSHint with Grunt to automate the linting of our JavaScript. JSHint is a community-driven code-quality tool for detecting errors and potential problems in JavaScript applications. It aids teams in standardizing their JavaScript coding styles. JSHint is a fork of JSLint and is slightly less opinionated than its parent. JSHint also provides the ability for developers to set flags to enable and disable certain rules. Since its release in 2011, JSHint has been adopted by engineers at Facebook, Twitter, and jQuery, to name a few.

Fortunately, there is an existing plug-in for integrating JSHint into our Grunt workflow. The plug-in, one of the core plug-ins, is called grunt-contrib-plugin. Listing 4-25 demonstrates an updated Gruntfile.js with configuration for JSHint.

Listing 4-25. Configuration for JSHint

```
jshint: {
  dist: {
    src: ['Gruntfile.js', 'app/js/**/*.js']
  }
}

// These plugins provide necessary tasks.
grunt.loadNpmTasks('grunt-contrib-jshint');

// Default task.
grunt.registerTask('default', [
  'clean',
  'useminPrepare',
  'sass',
  'bowerInstall',
  'autoprefixer',
  'jshint',
  'handlebars',
  'recess',
  'uncss',
  'copy',
  'cssmin',
  'concat',
  'requirejs',
  'rev',
  'usemin'
]);
```

As Listing 4-25 demonstrates, to integrate JSHint into our existing workflow is very simple. The grunt-contrib-jshint plug-in only requires a set of source files to analyze. It is important to note the order in which the tasks are run, jshint being executed before the handlebars task, as the output from the handlebars task will not pass all the JSHint rules. Figure 4-5 shows a sample Grunt configuration in which the ordering of the `jshint` and `handlebars` tasks has been reversed.

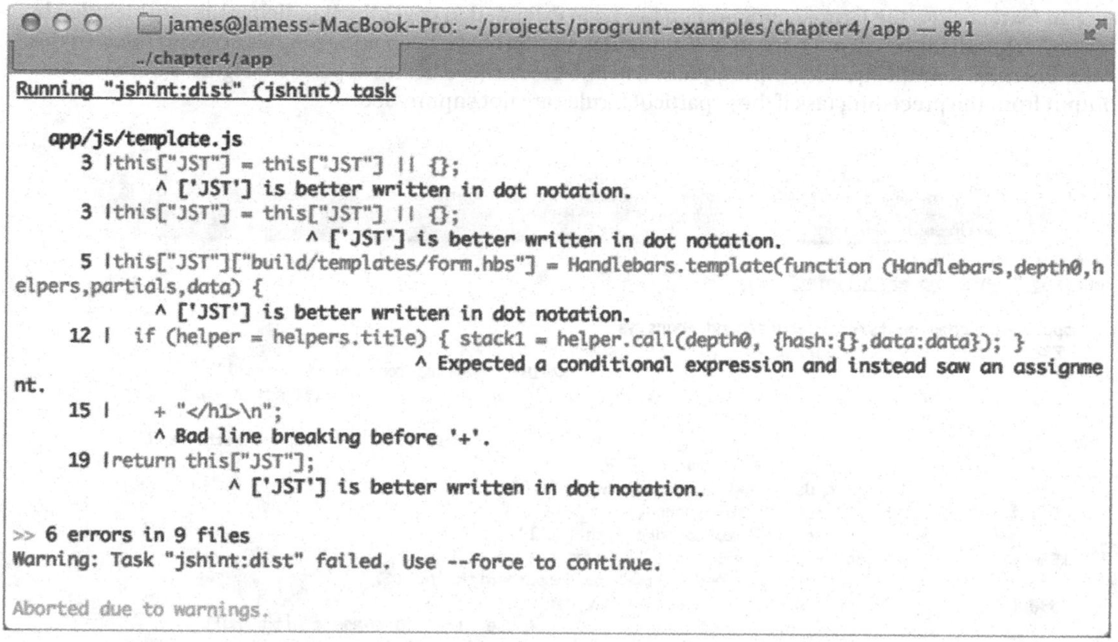

```
james@Jamess-MacBook-Pro: ~/projects/progrunt-examples/chapter4/app — ⌘1
../chapter4/app
Running "jshint:dist" (jshint) task

   app/js/template.js
      3 |this["JST"] = this["JST"] || {};
            ^ ['JST'] is better written in dot notation.
      3 |this["JST"] = this["JST"] || {};
                         ^ ['JST'] is better written in dot notation.
      5 |this["JST"]["build/templates/form.hbs"] = Handlebars.template(function (Handlebars,depth0,h
elpers,partials,data) {
            ^ ['JST'] is better written in dot notation.
     12 |  if (helper = helpers.title) { stack1 = helper.call(depth0, {hash:{},data:data}); }
                                  ^ Expected a conditional expression and instead saw an assignme
nt.
     15 |     + "</h1>\n";
            ^ Bad line breaking before '+'.
     19 |return this["JST"];
                 ^ ['JST'] is better written in dot notation.

>> 6 errors in 9 files
Warning: Task "jshint:dist" failed. Use --force to continue.

Aborted due to warnings.
```

Figure 4-5. *Reversing the ordering of tasks leads to errors*

With some applications, you may want to lint the JavaScript included via bower. This may produce errors, as highlighted in Figure 4-5, which can be resolved by modifying the rules applied by JSHint. There are three approaches to modifying the ruleset applied by JSHint whilse integrating with Grunt. The first opton is to apply the configuration via Grunt options; the second is to use a `.jshintrc` file; and the last option is to define your rulesets within your `package.json`. The first option is useful when you have to apply configuration via rulesets for different source files. For example, you can apply one set of rules of your application code while another set of libraries is developed by others. Listing 4-26 demonstrates this first approach.

Listing 4-26. Configuration Containing Options

```
jshint: {
  dist: {
    src: ['Gruntfile.js', 'app/js/**/*.js']
  },
  bower: {
    options: {
      "eqnull": true,
      "eqeqeq": true,
      "laxbreak": true,
    },
    src: ['app/bower_components/handlebars/handlebars.js']
  }
}
```

In Listing 4-26, the Grunt configuration has been extended to cover the handlebars library included by bower. As handlebars will not pass all of JSHint rules, options have been added to relax certain rules. In this case, the rules for null equality, triple equals, and line breaks have been suppressed. Figure 4-6 shows the output from the preceding task if these particular rules are not suppressed.

```
james@Jamess-MacBook-Pro: ~/projects/progrunt-examples/chapter4/app — ⌘1
~/chapter4/app
→ grunt jshint:bower
Running "jshint:bower" (jshint) task

   app/bower_components/handlebars/handlebars.js
    232 |      } else if(context === false || context == null) {
                                                   ^ Use '===' to compare with 'null'.
    311 |      var level = options.data && options.data.level != null ? parseInt(options.data.level,
 10) : 1;
                                                            ^ Use '!==' to compare with 'null'.
    386 |      if (result != null) { return result; }
                            ^ Use '!==' to compare with 'null'.
    584 |      if (open != null && open.charAt) {
                          ^ Use '!==' to compare with 'null'.
   1530 |         isBlock = program != null || inverse != null;
                                    ^ Use '!==' to compare with 'null'.
   1530 |         isBlock = program != null || inverse != null;
                                                      ^ Use '!==' to compare with 'null'.
   1707 |    if (input == null || (typeof input !== 'string' && input.constructor !== env.AST.Progra
mNode)) {
                      ^ Use '===' to compare with 'null'.
   1722 |    if (input == null || (typeof input !== 'string' && input.constructor !== env.AST.Progra
mNode)) {
                      ^ Use '===' to compare with 'null'.
   2242 |      if (guid != null) {
                      ^ Use '!==' to compare with 'null'.
   2272 |         + lookup
                 ^ Bad line breaking before '+'.
   2273 |         + ',helper '
                 ^ Bad line breaking before '+'.
   2274 |           + '? helper.call(' + helper.callParams + ') '
                   ^ Bad line breaking before '+'.
   2275 |           + ': helperMissing.call(' + helper.helperMissingParams + '))');
                   ^ Bad line breaking before '+'.
   2386 |        if (index == null) {
                          ^ Use '===' to compare with 'null'.
   2411 |      if(guid == null) {
                      ^ Use '===' to compare with 'null'.
```

***Figure 4-6.** Handlebars failing JSHint rules*

Another alternative approach to relaxing JSHint rules is to apply global runtime configuration. This requires creating a new file in the root of your project. This file should be named `.jshintrc`, and the contents should be formatted as valid JSON. The JSON object should contain a set of rules to be suppressed. An example of this is presented in Listing 4-27. For JSHint to use this file, the Grunt configuration requires an additional option setting. This option is `jshintrc`, which can either be set to `true` or as a path to a `jshintrc` file. In a case wherein you have options set within your Grunt file and a `.jshintrc`, the rulesets are not merged, and the `jshintrc` file configuration is used instead of the Gruntfile configuration.

Listing 4-27. JSHint Runtime Configuration

```
{
  "eqnull": true,
  "eqeqeq": true,
  "laxbreak": true
}
```

The final approach is similar to the use of a `.jshintrc` file. The modifications to be made to the ruleset are declared in the projects `package.json` under the property `jshintConfig`.

Modernizr

Modernizr is a popular feature-detection library written in JavaScript for determining which features from HTML5 and CSS3 specifications are available in the browser. It has become hugely popular within the development community, as it allows designers and developers to utilize the latest web technologies while ensuring that a good experience can be maintained for users with browsers that are lagging behind. Modernizr is a great tool to add to your toolbelt, especially when implementing progressive enhancements.

Modernizr runs quickly within the page, generating a JavaScript object and adding classes to the HTML element of the page that act as hooks within your CSS. Listing 4-28 demonstrates the use of the JavaScript object generated, while Listing 4-29 shows how Modernizr adds CSS classes to the HTML element.

Listing 4-28. Using Modernizr JavaScript to Detect `localStorage`

```
if (Modernizr.localstorage) {
  // use localstorage
} else {
  // use alternative storage
}
```

Listing 4-29. Modernizr Modifies HTML Elements, Providing Easy Hooks Within CSS

```
<html lang="en" class="js no-touch postmessage history multiplebgs boxshadow opacity
cssanimations csscolumns cssgradients csstransforms csstransitions fontface localstorage
sessionstorage svg inlinesvg no-blobbuilder blob bloburls download formdata">
```

The Modernizr team has produced a Grunt plug-in that mirrors the functionality of their Modulizr. The grunt-modernizr plug-in processes your JavaScript, CSS, and SCSS files to build an optimized version for your project. The optimized version of Modernizr will only contain tests for the features you use within your project. This helps to reduce the overall size of the JavaScript used in the production version of your applications, thereby reducing the page load time. Listing 4-30 shows a modified Gruntfile configuration for the grunt-modernizr plug-in.

Listing 4-30. Gruntfile Configuration for grunt-modernizr

```
modernizr: {
  dist: {
    devFile : "remote",
    outputFile : "app/js/modernizr.js",
    extra : {
      shiv : true,
      load : false,
```

```
        cssclasses : true
      },
      uglify : true,
      parseFiles : true,
      files : {
        src: ["build/styles/**/*.scss", "app/js/**/*.js"]
      }
    }
  }
```

The grunt-modernizr plug-in requires a development version of Modernizr, in order to produce an optimized version. In Listing 4-30, the option `devFile` is set to `remote`. This option is used to prevent false positives as the task runs. For example, if you had a local version of Modernizr installed and ran the task, there would be the potential for the file to be processed by the task, leading to an unoptimized version of Modernizr being generated. The next option, `outputFile`, tells the task where the optimized version of Modernizr should be output. The next option is labeled `extra`, which relates to the extras available on the Modernizr download page. The configuration in Listing 4-30 includes the `html5shiv` and support for adding CSS classes to the HTML element, while explicitly excluding `Modernizr.load`, which is a resource loader. The `parseFiles` option, coupled with the `files` option, configures the task to crawl the files within the project for refreshes to Modernizr features. Listing 4-31 contains a snippet of JavaScript that will cause the task to include support for testing whether the brower has support for `localStorage`.

Listing 4-31. JavaScript Snippet That Will Trigger the Browser to Include Modernizr Test for `localStorage`

```
if (Modernizr.localstorage) {
  var item = localStorage.getItem("favourite");
}
```

The next example, Listing 4-32, demonstrates how the task parses SCSS files, to determine which features to detect in the optimized Modernizr.

Listing 4-32. SCSS File Including a CSS Class That Matches Those Found in Modernizr

```
.profile {
  .boxshadow {
    box-shadow: 0px 0px 10px 1px rgba(0, 0, 0, 0.5);
  }
}
```

Next time the task runs, it will find the `boxshadow` class in the SCSS file and include the tests for box shadow.

Minification

So far in this chapter, we have focused heavily on optimizing our JavaScript code to ensure that our application is error-free and compressed. Owing to the use of `usemin`, we haven't had to explicitly configure a task to minify, as `usemin` automatically uses Uglify to minify and obfuscate the JavaScript. We will briefly look at how we can configure Grunt without the `usemin` task to minify JavaScript files.

A number of plug-ins exist for minifying JavaScript. To simplify things, we'll focus on using Uglify to minify and then obfuscate our JavaScript. There is a core plug-in available for integrating Uglify into a Grunt workflow. Listing 4-33 contains a sample configuration for the plug-in grunt-contrib-uglify.

Listing 4-33. Configuration for grunt-contrib-uglify

```
uglify: {
  options: {
    report: 'gzip'
  },
  dist: {
    files: {
      'dist/js/main.js': ['app/js/main.js']
    }
  }
}
```

The configuration in Listing 4-33 is fairly simple; it sets the report that the task should generate in terms of size, saving, and the files to operate on. The report option determines output from the task. Setting the option to gzip will print an additional size, which represents the size of the output JavaScript if it was to be compressed with gzip. In addition to the preceding, it would be a good idea to contact multiple files for production application. Again, this task is performed by the `usemin` task previously. By combining files, the rates of compression should be greater. Again, there is another core plug-in available for performing this task. The grunt-contrib-concat plug-in is available to concatenate multiple files into a single file. Listing 4-34 shows a sample configuration for this task.

Listing 4-34. grunt-contrib-concat Configuration

```
concat: {
  dist: {
    files: {
      'dist/js/main.js': ['app/js/**/*.js']
    }
  }
}
```

The preceding configuration will combine all JavaScript files and then store the output to the `dist` folder. At this stage, it would be a good practice to run the `Uglify` task over the file output from the `concat` task.

Documentation

In this final section, we will briefly explore how Grunt can be used to automate the production of documentation for JavaScript applications. Automating the production of documentation is important if you are producing libraries for other developers to consume. Without automation, the task of maintaining a solid set of documentation can become difficult and can lead to other developers becoming rapidly frustrated when they try to reuse the JavaScript library. There is a plug-in available for producing documentation. Known as grunt-jsdoc, this plug-in makes a `jsdoc` task available that generates documentation in an HTML format. Listing 4-35 contains a sample configuration for generating documentation for the project.

Listing 4-35. grunt-jsdoc Configuration for Generating HTML Documentation

```
jsdoc : {
  dist : {
    src: ['app/js/**/*.js'],
    options: {
      destination: 'doc'
    }
  }
}
```

Listing 4-35 is very simple, as it defines the source of all JavaScript files to parse for documentation and an option to configure the output directory in which the documentation will be created. To generate documentation, annotations have to be added to our JavaScript modules. Listing 4-36 shows the to-do model updated with some annotations to generate the documentation.

Listing 4-36. Modified To-Do Model with JSDoc Annotations

```
/**
 * @name Todo
 * @classdesc Todo Model
 * @author James Cryer
 * @exports Backbone.Model
 */
define(['backbone'], function(Backbone) {
  return Backbone.Model.extend({

  });
});
```

Listing 4-36 does not provide an exhaustive list of annontations that can be used. In addition to modules, individual functions within a module can also be annotated. Figure 4-7 illustrates the generated documentated for the module in Listing 4-36.

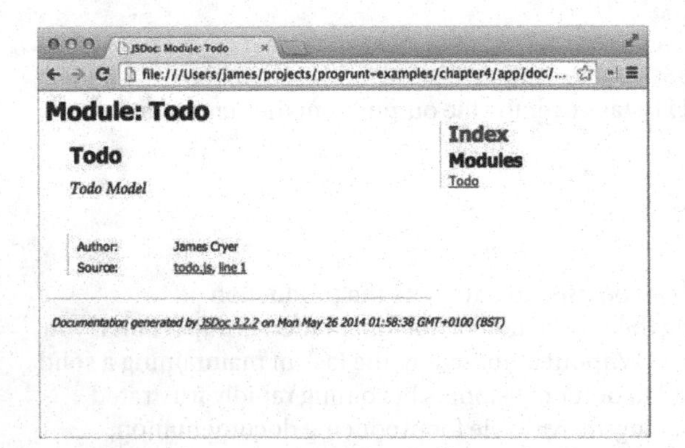

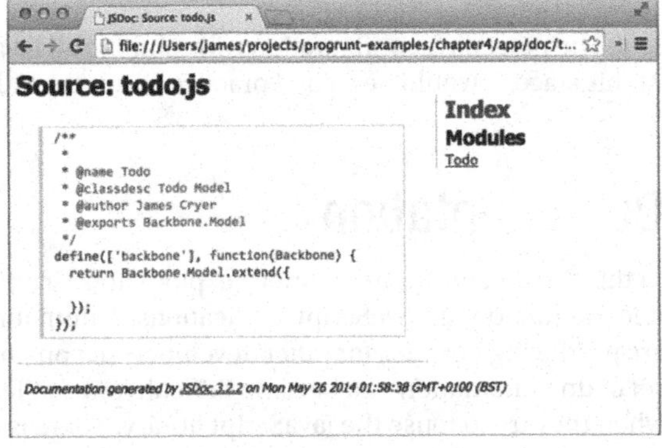

Figure 4-7. *JSDoc documentation automatically generated with Grunt*

Summary

In this chapter, I've covered how Grunt can optimize our JavaScript workflow with the use of JavaScript modules and templates. As part of this discussion, we've explored topics concerned with performance and ensuring that the production version of the JavaScript code is optimized for delivery to users. In addition to these topics, other tools were introduced, such as JSHint and Modernizr, to further enhance the development workflow with JavaScript. Finally, I concluded with a brief discussion on automating generation of documentation for complex JavaScript application.

The next chapter will focus on the workflow regarding visual elements of page, exploring the use of Grunt for automating tasks when working with imagery, web fonts, and SVG.

CHAPTER 5

Using Grunt with Images, SVG, and Icons

So far, we've explored how Grunt can be used to optimize working with HTML, CSS, and JavaScript. Next, we'll discover how Grunt can be used with another fundamental task of web development: producing visual assets. Since the start of the mobile revolution, the fall of Flash, and the emergence of high-density pixel displays, preparing visual assets for production has become more and more complicated. In this chapter, Grunt will be used to optimize images, producing multiple versions for different devices, and to minify SVG files. As always, using Grunt results in a powerful set of tools that can be used across many projects.

Compressing Images

The first topic that we will review in this chapter is image optimization. In this section, we will explore how Grunt can be used to optimize images ready for use within our applications. Image optimization is an important part of improving load-time performance of modern web applications, as images are typically a significant portion of a page's total weight. Optimization can be used to reduce the file size of images, without compromising image quality.

There are a number of factors to consider when using imagery within a web application. The initial question you need to answer is, Which format is correct to use for your image? There are two formats to consider: vector and raster images. I will discuss vector images in more depth later in this chapter, when reviewing the use of SVG (Scalable Vector Graphic) with Grunt. SVG is a vector format that can be used to generate highly scalable images, without an increase in file size. First, I'll focus on raster images.

Raster images have been more traditionally used on the Web, mainly due to browser vendor support. Raster images can be served in multiple formats, such as GIF, PNG, or JPEG. As the data for raster images are stored as a grid of pixels, they do not offer a scalable image format. As the image size increases, the file size will also increase. Each raster image format is typically used for a specific purpose. As outlined in Google's Web Fundamentals (`https://developers.google.com/web/fundamentals/media/images/optimize-images-for-performance`), JPEG images are usually used for photography and PNG for solid color graphics such as logos.

As noted throughout the book, when developing modern web applications, load-time performance can be critical to the success of our applications, as users have perceptions regarding page load times. Therefore, we must strive to deliver the most enhanced experience, while optimizing our pages to load rapidly. As imagery can play an important part of the general user experience, we must also consider how we can optimize these assets when developing our application. Optimization in this context means reducing the file size of the images while not compromising on image quality. Raster images can be dramatically reduced in file size, by passing them through tools that apply loseless and lossy compression.

Loseless compression takes its name from the fact that the original file can be re-created exactly; nothing is stripped from the file. Loseless compression is based on the concept of splitting the file into smaller parts, for transmission and/or storage. Lossy compression applies a different principle. With this form of compression, data is removed from the image, and the output cannot be used to re-create the original file. Grunt can be used to automate the use of these compression files within your application and also to report the percentage reduction of the file size for each image.

In this section, we will introduce a new plug-in: grunt-contrib-imagemin. This adds support for compressing GIF, JPEG, PNG, and SVG formats. For now, we will explore the use of this plug-in for raster images only. Let's start first by adding the new plug-in to our project (see Listing 5-1).

Listing 5-1. Adding grunt-contrib-imagemin to `package.json` Using npm

```
npm install grunt-contrib-imagemin --save-dev
```

Now that the plug-in has been installed for the project, next we must configure the plug-in to find our images and optimize each one. Listing 5-2 demonstrates a sample Gruntfile configuration for the newly added plug-in.

Listing 5-2. Gruntfile Configuration for grunt-contrib-imagemin

```
...
imagemin: {
  app: {
    options: {
      optimizationLevel: 6,
      progressive: true,
      use: [pngquant()]
    },
    files: [{
      expand: true,
      cwd: 'src/',
      src: ['**/*.{png,jpg,gif}'],
      dest: 'dist/'
    }]
  }
}
...
```

The options defined in the configuration within Listing 5-2 set the level of optimization to 6, conversion of JPEG compression to progressive, and, finally, the use of a plug-in known as pngquant. Let's explore each of these options individually.

We set an option known as `optimizationLevel` to the value of 6. The `optimizationLevel` option controls how many trials are run to compress the IDAT chunks of PNG images. This is primarily a feature of the PNG compression tool included with the plug-in, known as `optipng`. IDAT chunks are essentially the image data for a PNG file. The more trials run, the longer the compression will take, as more effort is needed as `optipng` attempts to find the optimal trial. Each trial will attempt to use a series of compression technics to reduce the file in size, without affecting the image quality. This option accepts values from `0` to `7`. A value of `0` means that no compression is applied to the files, and with a value of `7`, 240 trials will be run in an attempt to reduce the image in size.

The `progressive` option allows us to affect how `jpegtran`, the JPEG compression tool used by grunt-contrib-imagemin, is used. The `progressive` option can either be enabled or disabled. When this option is enabled with the value of `true`, the resulting JPEG file will be in a progressive JPEG format.

Progressive JPEGs render, as the name suggests, progressively. This means a low-quality version is initially visible, then, as more data is received over the network, the image quality will gradually improve. Progressive JPEGs can also boost better compression rates, if the original image is larger than approximately 30KB, studies have shown (`http://calendar.perfplanet.com/2012/progressive-jpegs-a-new-best-practice/`).

The final option we will look at is the `use` option. This allows the grunt-contrib-imagemin plug-in to be configured to use other imagemin plug-ins. Grunt-contrib-imagemin wraps the NodeJS module imagemin; therefore, any imagemin plug-in can be used with the plug-in as well. Altogether, there are ten plug-ins that can be used with imagemin. Each plug-in allows grunt-contrib-imagemin to use a series of compression tools. In our example, we've configured grunt-contrib-imagemin to use pngquant.

Before moving on to the next topic in this chapter, let's view a sample output for grunt-contrib-imagemin (see Figure 5-1). For this, we will add two new images to the project. One can be a large background image in a JPEG format and the other a delete icon that is a PNG image.

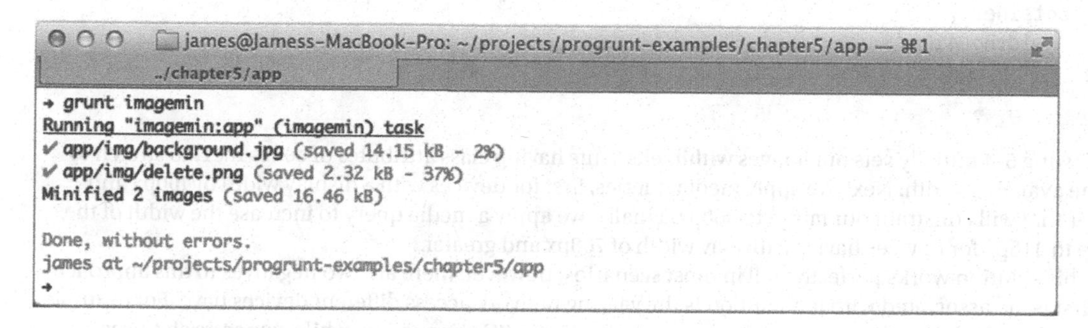

Figure 5-1. *grunt-contrib-imagemin sample output*

As shown in Figure 5-1, grunt-contrib-imagemin lists every file that is processed. For each file processed, the file source, the total size saved, and the percentage reduction are output. Finally, the total number is processed with the total reduction. Although image compression is an important part of an application build process, it does not tackle the problem of serving images for responsive sites. In the next section, we will use Grunt to prepare our imagery that is optimized for various breakpoints.

Producing Responsive Images

As discussed previously, the growth in the use of mobile devices is staggering. This introduces a new challenge, as, typically, mobile devices have smaller displays than traditional devices from which people have accessed web applications. Therefore, we need a solution to allow us to display an image across a breadth of devices. One that has become widely adopted since it was made popular after publication in *Responsive Web Design* by Ethan Marcotte (A Book Apart, 2011) is outlined in Listing 5-3.

Listing 5-3. Use of `max-width` to Ensure Images Fill Available Container Width While Maintaining Aspect

```
.container > img {
    max-width: 100%;
}
```

The CSS outlined in Listing 5-3 will ensure the image fills the available width within the element with the class attribute `.container`. Using the `max-width` property also ensures that the aspect ratio of the image is maintained as it fills the available width. This can then be coupled with media queries, introduced as part of the CSS3 standard, to render an image at different widths for each different class of devices. Listing 5-4 demonstrates the use of media queries to adjust the width of the image.

Listing 5-4. Use of Media Queries to Optimize the Display of Images

```
.container > img {
    max-width: 100%;
}

@media screen and (min-width: 400px) {
    .container {
        width: 368px;
    }
}

@media screen and (min-width: 768px) {
    .container {
        width: 416px;
    }
}
```

Listing 5-4 initially sets our images within elements having class attributes of `container`, to stretch to full the available width. Next, we apply media queries, first for devices with a display width of 400px and greater that will constrain our image to 368px. Finally, we apply a media query to increase the width of the image to 416px for devices having a display width of 768px and greater.

This solution works perfectly well in most scenarios; however, there are two negatives to this approach. The first issue associated with the solution is the varying network access different devices have. For example, some mobile devices may access your web application over a 3G connection, while someone else uses his/her home desktop device that employs a fiber broadband connection. Therefore, to ensure that the desktop experience is good, we have to use a large image and, thus, serve a high-resolution image. However, on a mobile device, the display size is a lot smaller, so we can afford to reduce the size of the image, to reduce page weight. The second issue associated with this solution is the performance impact. At the time of writing, image resizing performed by the browser is an expensive operation. The larger the image, the greater the cost of downsizing the image for a mobile display.

Resizing Images with Grunt

Let's tackle the second issue introduced, removing the need for a browser to resize an image to fit the device width. To solve this problem, we will produce images at a variety of breakpoints. The most appropriate image can then be used for each device. Producing multiple images each time we need to publish new content would be costly and is a repeatable task, therefore an ideal candidate for integration with our Grunt workflow. Let's introduce a new plug-in: grunt-responsive-images. This plug-in wraps the image processing tools GraphicsMagick and ImageMagick and allows a set of sizes by which to resize the original image. Listing 5-5 demonstrates installation of the plug-in.

Listing 5-5. Installing grunt-responsive-images

```
npm install --save-dev grunt-responsive-images
```

Before the plug-in can be used, GraphicsMagick or ImageMagick must be installed. For our examples, we will be using GraphicsMagick. To install GraphicsMagick, please visit the GraphicsMagick download page (`http://sourceforge.net/projects/graphicsmagick/files/graphicsmagick/`), for all platforms except Mac. Mac users can use Homebrew to install GraphicsMagick, as shown in Listing 5-6.

Listing 5-6. Installing GraphicsMagick with Homebrew

```
brew install GraphicsMagick
```

Next, the configuration for the plug-in has to be added to the project. Listing 5-7 demonstrates a sample configuration for the project.

Listing 5-7. Grunt Configuration for grunt-responsive-images

```
responsive_images: {
  dest: {
    options: {
      sizes: [{
        width: 320,
        height: 240
      },{
        name: 'large',
        width: 640
      },{
        name: "large",
        width: 1024,
        suffix: "_x2",
        quality: 60
      }]
    },
    files: [{
      expand: true,
      src: ['img/**.{jpg,gif,png}'],
      cwd: 'app/',
      dest: 'dist/'
    }]
  }
}
...
grunt.loadNpmTasks('grunt-responsive-images');
```

grunt-responsive-images is a very flexible plug-in that provides you with a lot of control over the outputted images. Let's break down the configuration from Listing 5-7, to explain how each works. First, we define our options, which are an array of sizes. Each size defines at least one dimension of the images to be output and will produce a new image at this size for each image passed the plug-in.

The first size used is the simplest possible example. We simply define a height and width for the image. This will result in a new image being generated with these dimensions and the file name suffixed with the new image dimensions. The second size option defines a single dimension, the width. This configuration will resize the image to match the specified dimension while maintaining the aspect ratio. This second set of configurations introduces a new option, `name`. The `name` option will be used as part of the image suffix. In our example, the new image file name will contain the original image name and the `name` suffix. An example would be `background-large.jpg`. The final configuration introduces two new options, `suffix` and `quality`. The `suffix` option allows an additional suffix to be appended to the file name and the name parameter. Our example in Listing 5-7 could produce an image of the final name `background-large_x2.jpg`. The quality parameter refers to quality of the JPEG image generated as part of the plug-in. This accepts values between 1 and 100, where 100 will produce the best-quality image.

In addition to these options, we also define a files configuration for our target. This is the standard Grunt file array format that will find all images in our `/app/img` directory, pass these to the plug-in, and store the output in `/dist/img`.

The grunt-responsive-image plug-in also allows the following to be defined in configuration:

- `rename`: This provides the ability to replace the image's original file name while maintaining its suffixes.
- `aspectRatio`: This option is maintained by default. Setting it to `false` does not maintain the aspect ratio.
- `gravity`: During the cropping of the image, this option controls where the image is placed. By default, this is set to center. It accepts values for all compass points (e.g., northwest, north, northeast, etc.).
- `upscale`: This determines whether an image should be upscaled if the dimensions are larger than the original image.
- `separator`: This is the character that is used between the file name and the suffix.
- `units`: This provides a mapping among pixels, percentages, and multiply units and their representation. By default, this option is set to `{ percentage: 'pc', pixel: '', multiply: 'x' }`.

Before moving on to how we can use these newly produced images in our application, we'll quickly look at the output of the plug-in, as demonstrated in Figures 5-2 and 5-3.

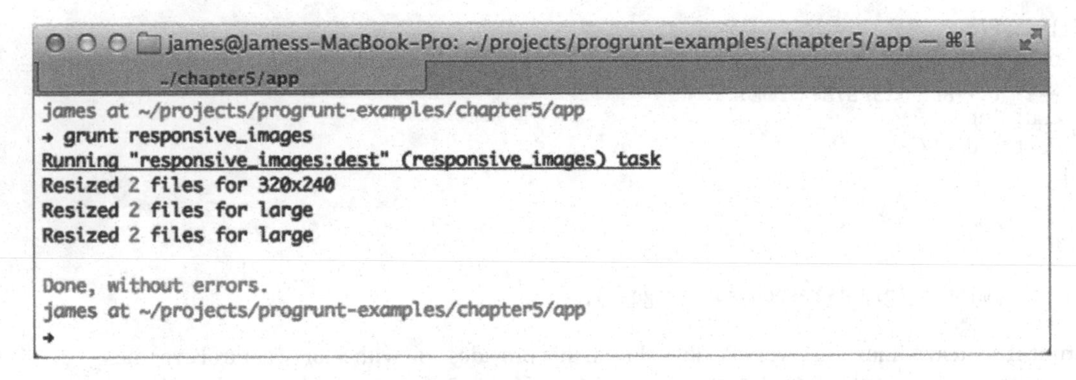

james@Jamess-MacBook-Pro: ~/projects/progrunt-examples/chapter5/app — ⌘1
~/chapter5/app
james at ~/projects/progrunt-examples/chapter5/app
→ grunt responsive_images
Running "responsive_images:dest" (responsive_images) task
Resized 2 files for 320x240
Resized 2 files for large
Resized 2 files for large
Done, without errors.
james at ~/projects/progrunt-examples/chapter5/app
→

Figure 5-2. *Sample output from grunt-responsive-images*

Name	Date Modified	Size	Kind
background-320x240.jpg	Today 04:50	78 KB	JPEG image
background-large_x2.jpg	Today 04:50	41 KB	JPEG image
background-large.jpg	Today 04:50	275 KB	JPEG image
background.jpg	Today 03:14	650 KB	JPEG image
delete-320x240.png	Today 04:50	3 KB	PNG image
delete-large_x2.png	Today 04:50	11 KB	PNG image
delete-large.png	Today 04:50	7 KB	PNG image
delete.png	Today 03:14	4 KB	PNG image

Figure 5-3. *Images produced by grunt-responsive-images*

As Figure 5-2 demonstrates, the plug-in will output the number of files generated for each size configuration. In our configuration, we had three different sets of images. This generated three lines of output, and for each set of size options, the plug-in produced two images. Figure 5-3 shows the images generated from the configuration in Listing 5-6 and listed in Figure 5-2. Two source images, background.jpg and delete.png, are transformed by the plug-in to produce three additional images for each image. Now that we have a series of images, we must apply these to the relevant devices.

Background images are easily applied using CSS. We can target devices at different widths using media queries. Listing 5-8 demonstrates an example of applying multiple versions of a background image for a different class of devices.

Listing 5-8. Applying Responsive Images Using Media Queries

```
body {
    background: url(../img/background-320x240.jpg);
}

@media screen and (min-width: 600px) {
    body {
        background: url(../img/background-large.jpg);
    }
}
```

Responsive Images with srcset

This solution works well for background images but does not solve the problem for images that appear in our content. At the time of writing, the `srcset` attribute for image elements is only supported in the latest version of Firefox, Chrome, Safari, and Opera. The `srcset` attribute allows developers to define multiple images' sources for different device attributes. Listing 5-9 demonstrates an example of this.

Listing 5-9. `srcset` Used to Define Different Images

```
<img alt="Cool Apps" src="del1x.jpg" srcset="del1x.jpg 1x, del2x.jpg 2x, del4x.jpg 4x">
```

The `srcset` attribute specification has been replaced with the picture element specification, which defines the picture element and extends the original `srcset` attribute. The specification details a richer set of attributes that can be used to target specific devices, in much the same way we can target CSS for particular devices. The picture element (see Listing 5-10), at the time of writing, is only supported in the latest version of Chrome and Firefox.

Listing 5-10. Picture Element

```
<picture>
   <source media="(min-width: 64em)" src="high-res.jpg">
   <source media="(min-width: 37.5em)" src="med-res.jpg">
   <source src="low-res.jpg">
   <img src="fallback.jpg" alt="This picture loads on non-supporting browsers.">
   <p>Accessible text.</p>
</picture>
```

To support a similar solution in older browsers, I'd suggest serving the lowest quality image and progressively enhancing the user experience through the use of JavaScript solutions. One such solution is Imager.js, produced by the BBC Responsive News team (`https://github.com/BBC-News/Imager.js/`).

Imager.js simplifies the workflow when working images for responsivity and prevents multiple images from being downloaded by the browser. Image elements are swapped with elements that have data attributes for the image source. They are called to Image.js then defined by the image widths available, allowing you to define pixel density as well. Image.js then runs over the page, replacing these elements with image elements most appropriate to the image. Listing 5-11 demonstrates the HTML before Image.js is run, while Listing 5-12 illustrates the effect of Imager.js on the HTML of the page.

Listing 5-11. HTML Before Imager.js

```
<div style="width: 240px">
    <div class="delayed-image-load" data-src="http://placehold.it/{width}"
data-alt="alternative text"></div>
</div>

<script>
    new Imager({ availableWidths: [200, 260, 320, 600] });
</script>
```

Listing 5-12. HTML After Imager.js Has Modified the Page

```
<div style="width: 240px">
    <img src="http://placehold.it/260" data-src="http://placehold.it/{width}"
alt="alternative text" class="image-replace">
</div>

<script>
    new Imager({ availableWidths: [200, 260, 320, 600] });
</script>
```

As demonstrated in Listing 5-12, Image.js has modified the original `div` element, replacing it with a new `img` element. From the array of available sizes, Image.js has chosen 260 for our current device. It replaces the placeholder, `{width}`, with the chosen width, before setting this as the `src` attribute for the new image element. As the images are also lazily loaded, the initial page render time should be improved as well.

This concludes the section on responsive images. Next, I'll introduce a new plug-in capable of generating image sprites.

Producing Image Sprites

This is the final section of our exploration of Grunt to automate image optimization for modern web applications. Image spriting is a performance technique that aims to reduce the number of HTTP requests made when rendering a page. An image sprite combines several smaller images into a single larger image. Although this does not necessarily reduce the amount of bandwidth used by the page, it can improve the performance of the load time of the page. Having multiple requests for images from the same domain can lead to a bottleneck in your page load time, as some browsers implement a limit on the number of requests that can be simultaneously made to the same domain. For example, Internet Explorer 10 restricts the number of parallel downloads for a single domain to eight requests. Therefore, if you have a lot of iconography on a page, this could lead to some icons taking longer than expected to be downloaded. Creating an image sprite can help resolve this issue, as a single request is made for the sprite, instead of a request per image.

The simplest yet most time-consuming method of generating a sprite is by hand. This means opening all your icons into your favorite image-editing software and carefully placing each image alongside one another before exporting the newly produced sprite as an optimized image. Once the sprite has been handcrafted, you will then have to produce the CSS that will be used to position the sprite correctly, so that only a single icon appears in the correct element. Each time you add a new icon or logo to your site, you will have to reopen the sprite and modify the CSS. Obviously, this isn't ideal and carries a lot of overhead in terms of maintenance. The maintenance is also doubled if you want to start producing a retina sprite sheet for devices with higher pixel density displays.

A second approach is to use a free online tool, such as `www.spritebox.net`, that provides convenient means for uploading and creating sprites. These online tools are more powerful than the manual approach described previously, as they often produce the CSS, LESS, or SASS for integrating into your application. The main drawback of using these tools is the need to be online to use them, and they don't seamlessly integrate with your workflow. If you have to work offline, you'll have to wait until you can get back online before updating your imagery and sprites. Also, as the images are generated online, you will have to optimize these, once you copy the new sprite into your project.

Automating Sprite Creation

The previous approaches are far from perfect, as outlined, but some of the shortfalls can be addressed by the use of Grunt. Using Grunt to generate the sprite has benefits of making the process repeatable and reusable. In addition to these, most Grunt plug-ins developed for sprite generation can be run offline. There are a number of sprite generation plug-ins available for Grunt. I will focus on one in particular, called grunt-spritesmith. This plug-in has a rich set of options that allows for full control over the sprite generated and also provides options to output CSS for most major CSS preprocessors. Listing 5-13 demonstrates how to install grunt-spritesmith to your project.

Listing 5-13. Installing grunt-spritesmith

```
npm install  grunt-spritesmith --save-dev
```

The plug-in works on the basis of using a sprite engine. A sprite engine is an external image-processing tool that the plug-in uses to process the sprite. The plug-in, at the time of writing, supports pngsmith, phantomjs, canvas, and GraphicsMagick as sprite engines. The choice of sprite engine affects the capabilities of the plug-in. For example, using pngsmith will prevent the plug-in from processing images that are not png files. While canvas offers the best performance when processing more than 100 sprites, it is only supported on the Linux platform. In our examples, we will be using phantomjs, which is capable of processing all image formats.

Let's start to explore the options available when generating a sprite with grunt-spritesmith. Listing 5-14 provides a sample configuration that we will go through in detail.

Listing 5-14. grunt-spritesmith Configuration

```
sprite: {
    app: {
      src: ['build/icons/**.png'],
      destImg: 'app/img/sprite.png',
      destCSS: 'build/styles/_sprite.scss',
      imgPath: '../img',
      algorithm: 'top-down',
      padding: 35,
      engine: 'phantomjs',
      cssFormat: 'scss'
    }
  }
```

As demonstrated in Listing 5-14, grunt-spritesmith provides a lot of flexibility for generating a sprite that will work for your particular use case. I'll review each of the options defined in Listing 5-14 and provide an explanation of the impact each has on the outputted sprite and CSS. The first option is simply one to define which files should be included in the sprite. In the example, we have added a new folder in the `build` folder that contains all our icons. The next option, `destImg`, determines the location and the file name of the sprite sheet produced. The third option determines the location and the file name of the CSS produced by the plug-in. In our example, we are looking to produce SCSS to integrate with our existing SCSS workflow. The option `imgPath` controls the image path that appears within the CSS produced. This is useful if your path is different from your build. In our case, the CSS and images are not in the same location in our build folder; therefore, we specify the image path, so that our images will be correctly loaded. The `algorithm` option controls how the images are laid out in the sprite generated. This option allows the images to be added from top to bottom, left to right, or diagonally. This is particularly useful when working on a responsive solution for which images may have to be laid out in a particular manner, to support varying device widths. As with the `algorithm` option, the `padding` option also controls the layout of the images within the sprite. `padding`, as the name suggests, controls the amount of padding around each icon. In our example, we've chosen to use 35px padding around each icon. This is useful when you have large elements that require background images applied, and you have to ensure that only a single icon appears as the background image icon. As discussed, grunt-spritesmith delegates the image creation to third-party image tools. The engine option controls which tool is used to produce the sprite. In Listing 5-14, `phantomjs` is used as the tool to create the sprite image. One of the most powerful features of grunt-spritesmith is the ability to output the CSS in a chosen format. In our example, we've specified SCSS; however, the plug-in supports LESS, SASS, Stylus, and CSS outputs.

The output from the configuration in Listing 5-14 is two assets: the sprite image and SCSS file. Figure 5-4 demonstrates the output files in the project directory.

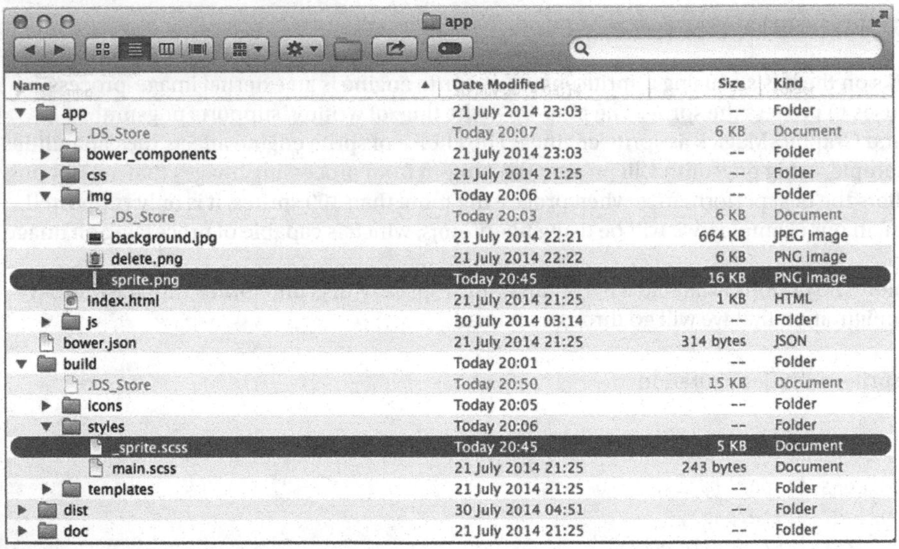

***Figure 5-4.** Sprite and SCSS files output from the grunt-spritesmith plug-in*

Another benefit of using grunt-spritesmith to produce the SCSS for your sprite sheet is the rich set of mixins produced. Listing 5-15 provides a sample of the overall SCSS file produced from the preceding example.

Listing 5-15. Sample SCSS Output from grunt-spritesmith

```
$upload-x: 0px;
$upload-y: 1443px;
$upload-offset-x: 0px;
$upload-offset-y: -1443px;
$upload-width: 76px;
$upload-height: 76px;
$upload-total-width: 76px;
$upload-total-height: 1741px;
$upload-image: '../img';
$upload: 0px 1443px 0px -1443px 76px 76px 76px 1741px '../img';

@mixin sprite-width($sprite) {
  width: nth($sprite, 5);
}

@mixin sprite-height($sprite) {
  height: nth($sprite, 6);
}

@mixin sprite-position($sprite) {
  $sprite-offset-x: nth($sprite, 3);
  $sprite-offset-y: nth($sprite, 4);
  background-position: $sprite-offset-x  $sprite-offset-y;
}

@mixin sprite-image($sprite) {
  $sprite-image: nth($sprite, 9);
  background-image: url(#{$sprite-image});
}

@mixin sprite($sprite) {
  @include sprite-image($sprite);
  @include sprite-position($sprite);
  @include sprite-width($sprite);
  @include sprite-height($sprite);
}
```

For each image added to the sprite sheet, grunt-spritesmith produces a number of variables prepended with the file name. Each variable contains a property for the image, for example, the x coordinate within the sprite sheet. These variables are combined and used by the mixins produced. There are also four mixins produced by the plug-in. The first four are convenience mixins that are used by the primary mixin, sprite. The sprite mixin is the mixin that can be used to actually produce CSS output that will contain the icon or image as background. Listing 5-16 demonstrates the use of the sprite mixin to add the upload icons to our CSS output.

Listing 5-16. Using grunt-spritesmith to Produce Icons in CSS

```
.icon-upload {
  @include sprite-width($icon-upload);
}
```

The creation of the various variables combined with the mixins produced by grunt-spritesmith makes maintaining your sprites incredibly easy. Any changes within the sprite itself are hidden from your SCSS, as the variable values changes do not require any updates within your own SCSS. In addition, the sprite and the SCSS can be passed through your other grunt tasks, leading to tasks such as linting and minification being applied.

Working with SVGs

The first part of this chapter has been dedicated to optimizing raster imagery for the Web. In the remainder of the chapter, I will focus on optimizing our workflow for dealing with SVG files. SVGs are excellent for producing lightweight icons that scale and can be styled using CSS. SVGs are an XML-based file format suitable for producing two-dimensional graphics in which elements are used to define paths, shapes, and polygons. Listing 5-17 demonstrates a basic SVG file, and Figure 5-5 illustrates the visual appearance of this SVG file.

Listing 5-17. Sample SVG Document

```
<?xml version="1.0" standalone="no"?>
<!DOCTYPE svg PUBLIC "-//W3C//DTD SVG 1.1//EN" "http://www.w3.org/Graphics/SVG/1.1/DTD/
svg11.dtd">
<svg xmlns="http://www.w3.org/2000/svg" width="39" height="32" viewBox="0 0 39 32">
    <!-- tick icon -->
    <path d="M15.815 32l23.475-28.046-4.695-3.954-19.521 23.228-11.12-9.266-1.954 10.695z"/>
</svg>
```

Figure 5-5. *The SVG visual output from Listing 5-17*

Along with basic two-dimensional graphics, JavaScript and CSS can be used with SVG to produce animations as well. This isn't the only feature of SVG that makes them desirable as a format of icons. The key benefit of using SVGs for icons is the fact that they are lightweight and can be easily scaled without affecting the quality of the image. The use of SVG files has increased over the past couple of years, primarily driven by the rise of people accessing the Web from a variety of devices. As SVGs are generally smaller in file size than raster images and, as stated previously, are easily scaled, this solves the problem of rendering sharp imagery for devices with high pixel density displays. However, as with all page assets, careful consideration should be taken not to bloat the page, adding page weight and producing a poor user experience. Grunt can help reduce the risk of this, by providing tools to automate optimization of SVG files.

Minifying SVG

As with CSS and JavaScript, SVG files can also be minified. This primarily derives from the fact that, as with other text-based file formats, unnecessary content and space can be stripped. This is particularly true if you export your SVG images from popular graphics packages. Luckily, Grunt has a plug-in available for optimizing SVG files that is ready for use within your application. The plug-in that I will introduce now is called grunt-svgmin. Grunt-svgmin wraps the Node.js library SVGO, an SVG optimizer. SVGO will perform optimizations such as removing empty attributes, comments, doctype declarations, and converting styles into attributes. Listing 5-18 shows a sample configuration for grunt-svgmin.

Listing 5-18. grunt-svgmin Configuration

```
svgmin: {
    app: {
      options: {
        plugins: [
          { removeViewBox: true },
          { removeUselessStrokeAndFill: true }
        ]
      },
      files: [{
        expand: true,
        cwd: 'build/svg',
        src: ['**/*.svg'],
        dest: 'app/img/',
        ext: '.min.svg'
      }]
    }
  }
```

The configuration shown in Listing 5-18 demonstrates the simplest of the configurations required to optimize SVG files within a project. There are two options defined: `removeViewBox` and `removeUselessStrokeAndFill`. The first of these options removes the `viewBox` attribute from the root SVG element. The second will remove strokes that have an accompanying `stroke-width` attribute set to `0` or none. If the SVG contains elements with the attribute `fill` set to none and the opacity set to `0`, then `fill-opacity` is removed. In addition, grunt-svgmin will also remove whitespace, comments, and doctype declarations from the SVG. Listing 5-19 shows a sample input SVG file, followed by the optimized version in Listing 5-20.

Listing 5-19. SVG File Before Optimization

```
<?xml version="1.0" standalone="no"?>
<!DOCTYPE svg PUBLIC "-//W3C//DTD SVG 1.1//EN" "http://www.w3.org/Graphics/SVG/1.1/DTD/
svg11.dtd">
<svg xmlns="http://www.w3.org/2000/svg" width="39" height="32" viewBox="0 0 39 32">
  <!-- tick icon -->
  <path stroke="0" stroke-width="0" fill="none" fill-opacity="0" d="M15.815 32l23.475-
28.046-4.695-3.954-19.521 23.228-11.12-9.266-1.954 10.695z"/>
</svg>
```

Listing 5-20. SVG File Optimized by grunt-svgmin

```
<svg xmlns="http://www.w3.org/2000/svg" width="39" height="32"><path d="M15.815 32L39.29
3.954 34.595 0l-19.52 23.228-11.12-9.266L2 24.657z" fill="none"/></svg>
```

The grunt-svgmin plug-in, as with other minification plug-ins, outputs the percentage reduction in file size after the minification has been applied. Figure 5-6 shows a sample output of the plug-in.

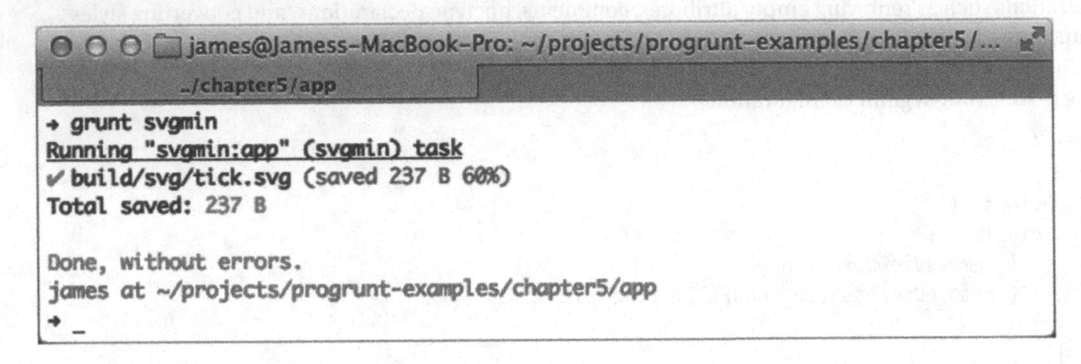

Figure 5-6. *Sample output from grunt-svgmin*

Generating SVG Sprites

There are a number of ways an SVG image can be included in a page, among them is using the object element, an iframe tag, a img tag, or embedding the content directly in the document. In addition to these methods, SVG files can also be references as backgrounds in CSS. As with all page assets, we have to attempt to reduce the number of requests required to download the whole page. This rule also applies to SVG files. Imagine a page with a lot of icons for a menu system. If each icon in the menu references an SVG file via an img element or is applied using a CSS background property, this could generate a number of unnecessary requests. As with raster images, we can combine SVG files into a single file and apply this instead of individual files. Doing so offers the benefits of have a single HTTP request for all images, and the SVG sprite can be compressed using gzip, offering further bandwidth reductions. To achieve these improvements, we can introduce a new plug-in called grunt-svg-sprite. Listing 5-21 demonstrates some sample configuration for grunt-svg-sprite.

Listing 5-21. grunt-svg-sprite Configuration

```
svgsprite: {
  app : {
    options: {
      render: {
        scss: {
          dest: '../../build/styles/_font.scss'
        },
        css: false
      },
      spritedir: '',
      padding: 35,
      layout: 'vertical'
    },
```

```
      src: 'build/svg/',
      dest: 'app/img/'
    }
  }
```

The configuration outlined in Listing 5-21 will generate an SVG sprite and an accompanying SCSS file. To achieve this, the `render` option has been set with a destination for the SCSS file. It should be noted that this path is relative to the destination directory defined by the `dest` option. Also, to disable CSS output, the `css` option has to be set to `false`. The next option defined, `spritedir`, prevents the sprite from being placed within a dedicated folder. In our example, the generated sprite will be output in the root of the `dest` folder. The `padding` option is the same as the grunt-spritesmith `padding` option. It controls the padding to apply around each icon. The final option supplied is `layout`. This controls how each icon is laid out in the SVG sprite. This accepts values of `vertical`, `horizontal`, or `diagonal`.

The SVG sprite can easily be integrated into our existing SASS workflow, by adding an import to the top of the `main.scss` file, as demonstrated in Listing 5-22.

Listing 5-22. Adding an SVG Sprite to a SASS File

```
@import 'font;
```

The compiled CSS will now have new CSS selectors defined, one for each icon included in the sprite. To use one of these icons, we can create HTML, as shown in Listing 5-23.

Listing 5-23. Demonstrating Using the SVG Sprite

```
<div class="svg-circle"></div>
```

The HTML in Listing 5-23 will apply the CSS background property to the `div` element that will render the icon corresponding to the originating `circle.svg` file.

Generating Icon Fonts

Before concluding this chapter, we will investigate how Grunt can be used to generate web fonts to support scalable icons for Internet Explorer 9 and later versions. Icon fonts have become a popular approach to applying icons to pages that works for both standard pixel density screens and higher pixel density displays. There are a number of sites that offer free resources, such as Font Awesome; however, choosing a large icon font can have a negative impact on a user's experience, as the icon can take a long time to download and only a small percentage of the whole font is used. The optimum approach is to create a font that contains only the icons that your application or site will use and save valuable bandwidth. Grunt has a plug-in available for creating a font from a series of SVG files. The plug-in is called grunt-webfont. Listing 5-24 demonstrates a sample configuration for grunt-webfont.

Listing 5-24. grunt-webfont Configuration

```
webfont: {
  icons: {
    options: {
      font: 'custom',
      stylesheet: 'scss',
      relativeFontPath: '../fonts',
      htmlDemo: false
    },
```

```
    destCss: 'build/styles/',
    src: 'build/svg/**/*.svg',
    dest: 'app/fonts'
  }
}
```

The configuration in Listing 5-24 defines a number of options similar to those of grunt-spritesmith, as grunt-webfont is capable of producing CSS, SCSS, or LESS in much the same way. The first option defines the name of the font to be produced. Second, the type of CSS produced is controlled by the `stylesheet` option. This accepts values of `css`, `less`, `sass`, and `scss`. The next option, `relativeFontPath`, controls the path to the font defined in CSS output. By default, grunt-webfont produces a demonstration HTML file that loads the font. Setting this option to `false` prevents the HTML demonstration file from being generated. The location of the CSS can be controlled by setting the option `destCss`. The `destCss` option accepts the directory in which the generated CSS will be placed. The final two options in our configuration determine which SVG files are included in our font and the location in which the generated font is placed.

As the plug-in creates the font, it outputs the number of glyphs that have been selected for a given font. This is shown in Figure 5-7.

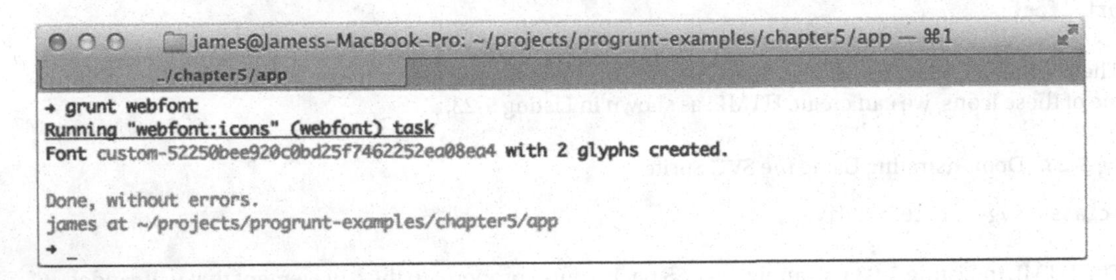

Figure 5-7. grunt-webfont sample output

Summary

In this chapter, I've covered how Grunt can be utilized to perform the repetitive and time-consuming tasks of generating optimized visual assets for web sites. In the first half the chapter, we looked at a variety of plug-ins for working raster images, before moving on to vector-based graphics such as SVG. This chapter has focused heavily on reducing page weight through combining and compressing visual assets, in an aim to booster performance in our production applications.

The next chapter will focus on using Grunt to create a web server for viewing and testing our applications locally.

CHAPTER 6

Using Grunt for Testing and Local Development

In previous chapters, we've concentrated on how to automate the build process, to optimize our assets and ensure they meet certain quality standards. In this chapter, we will focus on using Grunt to set up a local web server. Once set up, we'll explore using our local web server to perform tests that run in headless and actual browsers. To further ensure that the software we're building meets best practices of modern development, we'll expose our development environment to the Internet, which will allow us to automate the running of performance tests.

Setting Up a Local Server

As Grunt is built on top of the npm environment, setting up local web servers is trivial, as there are a number of npm packages available for creating them. Making it even easier, there are a number of Grunt plug-ins available to automate the starting of local web servers. There are plug-ins for starting servers, using popular web frameworks such as Flash (Python), Sinatra (Ruby), and Express (Node). In this chapter, we will be using grunt-contrib-connect. This plug-in wraps the npm packages `connect` and `connect-livereload` to provide a versatile local development environment for static publishing. Static publishing, in this context, refers to the process of dynamically generating assets to a static file for use in development or production.

To get started, we must first add grunt-contrib-connect to our project. As with all Grunt plug-ins, this is a simple npm install command, as shown in Listing 6-1.

Listing 6-1. Installing grunt-contrib-connect

```
npm install grunt-contrib-connect --save-dev
```

Once the plug-in has successfully been added to the project, we next configure our local web server, by defining configuration in our `Gruntfile.js` file. Listing 6-2 provides a sample configuration for setting up a simple HTTP server. We will explore setting up an HTTPS server later in the chapter. The configuration in Listing 6-2 will start a local web server running on port 8000, responding to any hostname, with the root of the web server being our application folder, called `app`. To start the web server, you have to run `grunt`, as shown in Listing 6-3, and you should see a similar output in the terminal as in Figure 6-1. If you now open your browser and try to access a web server configured on port 8000 (visiting `http://localhost:8000`), you will find that the web server is unavailable. You may have noticed that once the web server starts, Grunt exits. As Grunt exits, the connect web server is also shut down. grunt-contrib-connect can be used in conjunction with other plug-ins, such as grunt-contrib-jasmine, to automate running tests. Once the tests have been run, the web server can be shut down. However, when developing locally or debugging an issue in the browser, it is handy to keep the web server running. We will now update our configuration, to allow us to keep our server running continuously.

Listing 6-2. Configuring Connect to Run a Local Web Server

```
connect: {
    server: {
      options: {
        port: 8000,
        protocol: 'http',
        hostname: '*',
        base: './app'
      }
    }
  }
```

```
jamescryer@Jamess-MacBook-Pro: ~/projects/progrunt-examples/chapter...
→ grunt connect:server
Running "connect:server" (connect) task
Started connect web server on http://0.0.0.0:8000

Done, without errors.
james at ~/projects/progrunt-examples/chapter6/app
→
```

Figure 6-1. *Connecting, starting, and stopping a local web server*

Listing 6-3. Starting a Web Server with grunt-contrib-connect

```
grunt connect:server
```

Keeping the Server Running

To allow us to run a server that does not exit immediately, we have to modify our configuration to include the option `keepalive`. In Listing 6-4, we define an additional configuration for another web server that can be run for local development.

Listing 6-4. Configuring `connect` to Run a Local Web Server for Development

```
connect: {
    dev: {
      options: {
        port: 8001,
        protocol: 'http',
        hostname: '*',
        base: './app',
        keepalive: true
      }
    }
  }
```

Running the preceding task should produce an output like that demonstrated in Figure 6-2. It is important to note that in our second web server, we've configured it to run on port 8001. This will allow us to later run our tests against our server on port 8000, while allowing our development server to continue to run. As expected, if you try to bind two web servers to the same port number, the second will fail to start (Figure 6-3). This is important to remember later, when we have tests running in the background when a file changes.

```
grunt connect:dev — grunt — node — 93×7
james at ~/projects/progrunt-examples/chapter6/app
→ grunt connect:dev
Running "connect:dev" (connect) task
Waiting forever...
Started connect web server on http://0.0.0.0:8001
```

***Figure 6-2.** Running a local web server indefinitely*

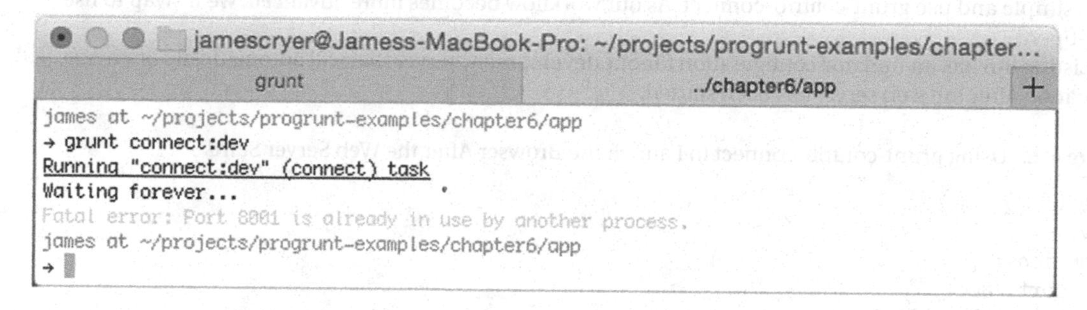

***Figure 6-3.** Attempting to run two web servers on the same port number*

If you now visit `http://localhost:8001` in your browser, you should see our application running. To stop the web server, we have to press Ctrl+C.

A common development pattern is to set up a development server with a Grunt task called `serve`. This is the pattern adopted by the Yeoman team and can be found in many of the generators for projects, such as Backbone.js. The `serve` task typically builds all the development assets, launches a web server, and then opens a browser for the application. Listing 6-5 contains the configuration for a sample `serve` task.

The task defined in Listing 6-5 is a little verbose for demonstration purposes. As your project matures, it is best to start to break down tasks into groups, as it communicates to other team members what each stage of the build is achieving without having to know the details of each individual stage. We'll be exploring how to optimize your build process in the next chapter.

Listing 6-5. Sample `serve` Task for Building and Launching a Development Environment

```
grunt.registerTask('serve', [
  'clean',
  'useminPrepare',
  'sass',
  'bowerInstall',
  'autoprefixer',
```

```
    'jshint',
  'modernizr',
  'handlebars',
  'imagemin',
  'uncss',
  'copy',
  'cssmin',
  'concat',
  'requirejs',
  'rev',
  'usemin',
  'connect:dev'
]);
```

Automated Browser Launching

One step missing from the task defined in Listing 6-5 is the automated opening of the browser. This can be achieved by either using grunt-open or grunt-contrib-connect. For our current workflow, we will keep things simple and use grunt-contrib-connect. As our workflow becomes more advanced, we'll swap to use grunt-open.

Listing 6-6 has an updated configuration for our development server that will automatically open our application after the web server has been started.

Listing 6-6. Using grunt-contrib-connect to Launch the Browser After the Web Server Starts

```
connect: {
  dev: {
    options: {
      port: 8001,
      protocol: 'http',
      hostname: '*',
      base: './app',
      keepalive: true,
      open: true
    }
  }
}
```

Adding the option open and setting the value to `true` will lead to your default browser automatically opening your application immediately after the web server has started.

Logging Requests to Our Server

With the current configuration, we cannot see requests being sent to our web server, because logging is not enabled by default. While developing locally, it can be handy to see which requests have been made successfully, the HTTP response code, and the time taken to generate the response. Fortunately, grunt-contrib-connect has this feature available. To enable logging, we have to set the debug option to `true`, as shown in Listing 6-7. Figure 6-4 provides a sample output from our application for the initial page load.

Listing 6-7. Adding Debug Option to Development Server Configuration

```
dev: {
  options: {
    port: 8001,
    protocol: 'http',
    hostname: '*',
    base: './app',
    keepalive: true,
    open: true,
    debug: true
  }
}
```

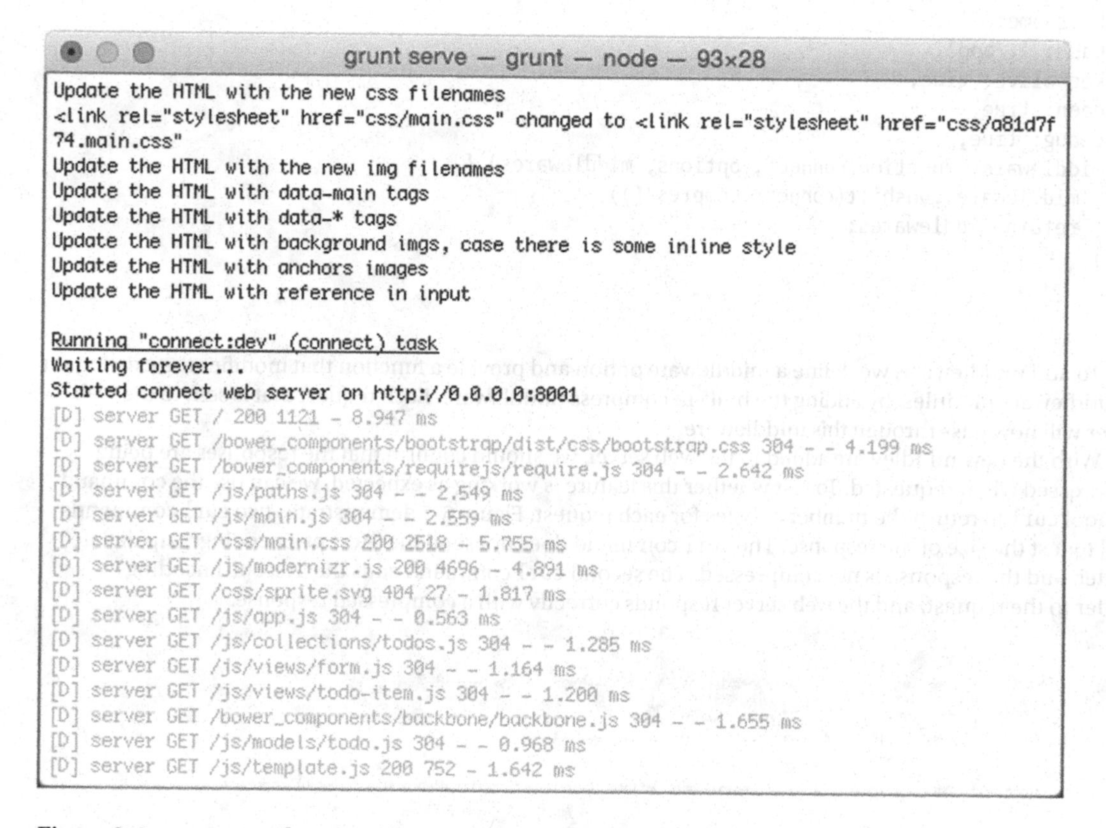

Figure 6-4. *grunt-contrib-connect logging requests sent to web server*

Extending Our Server with Compressed Responses

Now that we have our web server running, automatically opening and logging each request to our terminal, let's explore extending our web server with new features. As grunt-contrib-connect wraps the Node module connect, at the time of writing, version 2.x, we can extend our connect server with all the available middleware plug-ins (`https://github.com/senchalabs/connect/wiki`). There is middleware available for features such as BasicAuth, OAuth, and caching. In our example, we'll look to use one of the built-in middleware features: `compression`. This will dynamically server gzipped content, if the client sends the correct headers in the request. As grunt-contrib-connect wraps version 2.x of `connect`, the compression middleware is part of `connect`. In the latest version of `connect`, the core middleware features have been migrated to their own modules.

Listing 6-8 modifies our existing development web server configuration to support compression of our server responses.

Listing 6-8. Adding Middleware to Support Compression

```
dev: {
  options: {
    port: 8001,
    protocol: 'http',
    hostname: '*',
    base: './app',
    keepalive: true,
    open: true,
    debug: true,
    middleware: function(connect, options, middlewares) {
      middlewares.unshift(connect.compress());
      return middlewares;
    }
  }
}
```

To add middleware, we define a middleware option and provide a function that modifies the existing set of middleware modules, by adding the built-in compress middleware. Each request that is sent to the web server will now pass through this middleware.

With the new middleware added to the web server, we should confirm that the responses are being compressed when requested. To test whether this feature is working as expected, we can use the command-line tool `curl` to return the number of bytes for each request. Figure 6-5 demonstrates two `curl` commands used to test the size of the response. The `curl` command does not send the "Accept-Encoding: gzip,deflate" header, and the response is not compressed. The second `curl` command adds the "Accept-Encoding" header to the request, and the web server responds correctly with a compressed response.

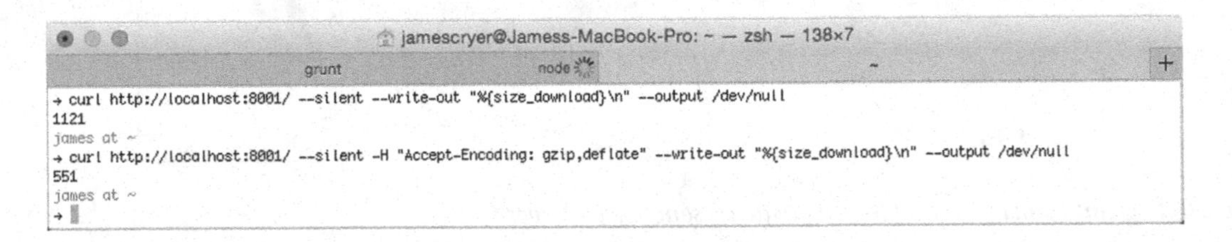

Figure 6-5. *Testing whether our middleware has been loaded as expected*

At this point, we have a robust local development server and another test server ready for integration with a test runner. We have the ability to run our application locally and even compress the response, as we'd want in production. In the next chapter, I will introduce the ability to automatically reload assets in the browser each time a file is modified on disk, without needing the ability to reload or refresh the browser. Next, we will start to automate testing our application in a variety of ways: unit, integration, accessibility, and performance.

Testing

In addition to running a local development server, we can automate the running of tests using Grunt. There is no denying the benefits of having a good suite of tests for an application. Tests can help prevent issues being released to production, act as a communication tool between team members, reduce risk when making changes to a complex application, and they are repeatable. A suite of automated tests can also dramatically reduce the time needed to verify an application required to run across multiple devices, as the test suite can be run in parallel on several devices. This is particularly relevant for responsive web applications.

Grunt can automate testing at all levels, from unit to system testing. In the next few sections, we'll explore setting up Grunt tasks to run unit tests, run tests in different browsers, validate the accessibility of our application, and, finally, conduct performance testing as well.

Writing Our First Test

Let's begin our journey into using Grunt to automate a variety of tests against our application by starting simply and writing tests for the smallest possible unit of our application. There are a variety of test frameworks available. For this particular example, we'll be using `nodeunit`. `Nodeunit` is a simple but robust test framework that allows tests to run asynchronously and support multiple reporting formats. There is a Grunt plug-in available that wraps the nodeunit package called grunt-contrib-nodeunit. Listing 6-9 illustrates adding the plug-in to the project.

Listing 6-9. Installing grunt-contrib-nodeunit

```
npm install --save-dev grunt-contrib-nodeunit
```

Next, the task configuration has to be added to our `Gruntfile.js` file (see Listing 6-10).

Listing 6-10. Configuration for grunt-contrib-nodeunit

```
nodeunit: {
    all: ['test/*_test.js'],
    options: {
      reporter: 'junit',
      reporterOptions: {
        output: 'out'
      }
    }
  }
```

The configuration in Listing 6-10 defines a target that will look for files within the test folder that end in `test.js`. For example, `item_test.js`, `list_test.js`, and `user_test.js` would all match the pattern if the files existed in the test folder. Additional configuration options have been set to configure the output of the test runner. The test runner in this instance has been configured to output the results, using the JUnit formatter, and the output should be stored in the directory `out`.

If the task is now run, we will get an output similar to the one shown in Figure 6-6, as we do not currently have a test folder or any tests written. Next, we will create a simple JavaScript module that represents an item in our to-do list. Listing 6-11 contains the definition of the to-do item module that extends the Backbone Model module.

Figure 6-6. Running grunt-contrib-nodeunit with no tests defined

Listing 6-11. A Simple JavaScript Module That Represents a To-Do Item

```
/**
  *
  * @name Todo
  * @classdesc Todo Model
  * @author James Cryer
  * @exports Backbone.Model
  */
'use strict';

var Backbone = require('backbone');

module.exports = Backbone.Model.extend({
  defaults: {
    'title': '',
    'date': '19/02/2015',
    'complete': false
  },

  complete: function () {
    this.set('complete', true);
  }
});
```

The “Todo” module defines a set of defaults: `title`, `date`, and `completion` status. There is also a single function defined to mark an instance of the Todo module as being complete. The Backbone Model module provides the ability to easily define default values for attributes for each instance of our Todo module.

The complete function uses the `set` function provided by the Backbone Model to modify attributes of our instances of the Todo module. Listing 6-12 provides an example of how this simple module could be used within an application. The trivial example creates a new instance of the Todo module, passing in the title and date it has to be completed by. After the to-do item is created, we set it as being complete. At the moment, we do not have a method of validating that our new Todo module is behaving as expected, unless we run it in the browser. Let’s use `nodeunit` combined with grunt-contrib-nodeunit to write a test that can be run each time we make a change to our module.

Listing 6-12. Example of Using the Todo Module

```
define([
  'js/model/todo'
], function (Todo) {
  var todo = new Todo({
    'title': 'buy groceries',
    'date': '20/02/2015'
  });
  todo.complete();
});
```

To create our first test, we must first create a new folder in the root of our application. It can often prove useful to create a mirror structure in your test folder that matches the application code. To keep our test folder structure in synchronization with our application folder, it is best to create a `models` folder within the newly created `test` folder. Inside the `models` folder, we'll create our first set of tests for our Todo module. The file should be named `todo_test.js`, so that it matches the pattern defined in our Grunt configuration. Listing 6-13 contains the contents of the test module.

Listing 6-13. Our First Test: Confirming That the Todo Module Is Functioning As Expected

```
'use strict';

    exports.todo = {
      setUp: function (done) {
        var Todo = require('../../app/js/models/todo');

        this.todo = new Todo({
          'title': 'Test Item',
          'date': '24/02/2014'
        });
        done();
      },
      item_has_a_title: function (test) {
        test.equal(this.todo.get('title'), 'Test Item');
        test.done();
      },
      item_is_not_complete: function (test) {
        test.equal(this.todo.get('complete'), false);
        test.done();
      },
      item_can_be_completed: function (test) {
        this.todo.complete();
        test.ok(this.todo.get('complete'));
        test.done();
      }
    };
```

The test module shown in Listing 6-13 contains a total of three tests: to ensure that an item has a title, that an item defaults to being incomplete, and a final test to ensure that an item can be marked as completed. If you now run the `nodeunit` task, as shown in Figure 6-7, you will see that there is a total three assertions made. Assertions should not be confused with tests; each test can have a number of assertions.

It is often considered best practice to make only one assertion per test; however, this is not a golden rule but more a principle to encourage writing tests that only test a small unit of the system. For example, in our test module, we have split the test for ensuring that the `complete` attribute is set to `true` after the `complete` function is called. We could have combined this with the previous test of checking the value of the `complete` attribute to `false`. However, by combining these tests, if either the default changed or the `complete` function broke, it would be harder to discover the cause of the issue.

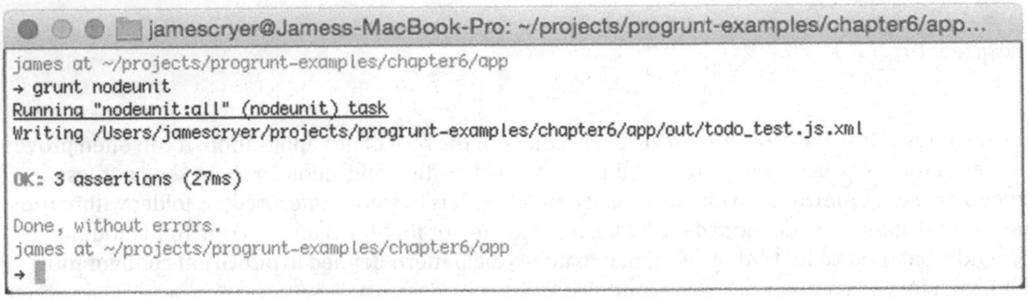

```
jamescryer@Jamess-MacBook-Pro: ~/projects/progrunt-examples/chapter6/app...
james at ~/projects/progrunt-examples/chapter6/app
→ grunt nodeunit
Running "nodeunit:all" (nodeunit) task
Writing /Users/jamescryer/projects/progrunt-examples/chapter6/app/out/todo_test.js.xml

OK: 3 assertions (27ms)

Done, without errors.
james at ~/projects/progrunt-examples/chapter6/app
→
```

Figure 6-7. *Running the `nodeunit` tests using `grunt`*

Modifying the Output from Nodeunit

The output from grunt-contrib-nodeunit is minimal, showing that, overall, the tests passed, the number of assertions run, and the time taken to complete the tests. As we currently have the JUnit reporter selected, the plug-in also outputs the location of the files containing the test results. Listing 6-14 contains the output generated from running grunt-contrib-nodeunit on the project.

Listing 6-14. Sample JUnit Reporter Output from grunt-contrib-nodeunit

```
<?xml version="1.0" encoding="UTF-8" ?>
<testsuite name="todo_test.js"
           errors="0"
           failures="0"
           tests="3">
  <testcase name="todo - item_has_a_title"></testcase>
  <testcase name="todo - item_is_not_complete"></testcase>
  <testcase name="todo - item_can_be_completed"></testcase>
</testsuite>
```

The output generated from running the plug-in can be used within a continuous integration environment. We will explore setting up such an environment later in this chapter.

Test-Driven Development with Grunt

Now that we have our first set of tests written, let's explore how easier it becomes to add new features to our Todo module. In this section, we'll explore using the testing methodology of writing our automated tests first, before writing a small amount of code to make our tests pass. Once we have our tests passing, we are free to re-factor our implementation to meet our development standards. This process is known as Test Driven Development and is often shortened to TDD. For example, let's add the ability to undo the completion of an item. Listing 6-15 illustrates the newly added function that is intended to mark an item as being incomplete.

Listing 6-15. A Simple JavaScript Module That Represents a To-Do Item

```
/**
  *
  * @name Todo
  * @classdesc Todo Model
  * @author James Cryer
  * @exports Backbone.Model
  */
'use strict';

var Backbone = require('backbone');

module.exports = Backbone.Model.extend({
  defaults: {
    'title': '',
    'date': '19/02/2015',
    'complete': false
  },

  complete: function () {
    this.set('complete', true);
  },

  undo: function () {
    this.set('complete', true);
  }
});
```

Next, we have to add a test to verify that the undo function is working as expected. This is shown in Listing 6-16.

Listing 6-16. Updating the Test Module to Verify the undo Function Is As Expected

```
'use strict';

exports.todo = {
  setUp: function (done) {
    var Todo = require('../../app/js/models/todo');

    this.todo = new Todo({
      'title': 'Test Item',
      'date': '24/02/2014'
    });
    done();
  },
  ...
```

```
  item_can_be_marked_as_incomplete: function (test) {
    this.todo.complete();
    this.todo.undo();
    test.equal(this.todo.get('complete'), false);
    test.done();
  }
};
```

Rerunning our tests should cause a failure, as we currently have a defect in the undo function. At present, it is setting the `complete` attribute to `true`, while it should be set to `false`. Figure 6-8 shows the output of rerunning the tests, with the failing test present.

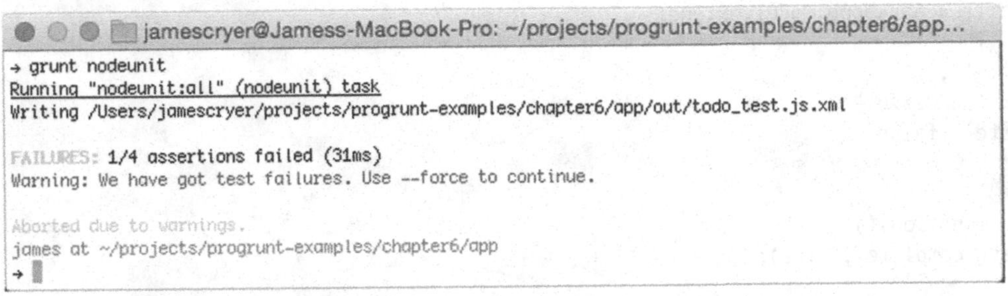

```
jamescryer@Jamess-MacBook-Pro: ~/projects/progrunt-examples/chapter6/app...
→ grunt nodeunit
Running "nodeunit:all" (nodeunit) task
Writing /Users/jamescryer/projects/progrunt-examples/chapter6/app/out/todo_test.js.xml

FAILURES: 1/4 assertions failed (31ms)
Warning: We have got test failures. Use --force to continue.

Aborted due to warnings.
james at ~/projects/progrunt-examples/chapter6/app
→
```

Figure 6-8. *grunt-contrib-nodeunit reporting a failing test*

If you open the test results file generated by the plug-in, it will provide you with a more detailed output of the cause of the failure. Alternatively, if you want to see the output in the console, the default reporter will output any errors generated by `nodeunit`, as shown in Figure 6-9.

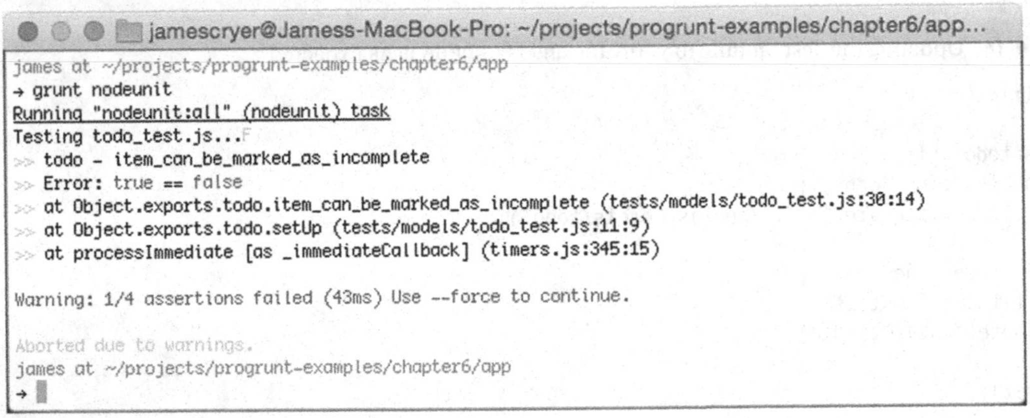

```
jamescryer@Jamess-MacBook-Pro: ~/projects/progrunt-examples/chapter6/app...
james at ~/projects/progrunt-examples/chapter6/app
→ grunt nodeunit
Running "nodeunit:all" (nodeunit) task
Testing todo_test.js...F
>> todo - item_can_be_marked_as_incomplete
>> Error: true == false
>> at Object.exports.todo.item_can_be_marked_as_incomplete (tests/models/todo_test.js:30:14)
>> at Object.exports.todo.setUp (tests/models/todo_test.js:11:9)
>> at processImmediate [as _immediateCallback] (timers.js:345:15)

Warning: 1/4 assertions failed (43ms) Use --force to continue.

Aborted due to warnings.
james at ~/projects/progrunt-examples/chapter6/app
→
```

Figure 6-9. *Failing test output to console*

The output generated from a failing test is informative, providing the file the test failed within, the name of the test, the reason for failure, and the line number, which further supports the principle of minimizing the number of things tested. A succinct test is usually far easier to understand and trace the cause of the failure. In our example, the cause of the failure is simply a matter of setting a value to `true` instead of `false`. If the `undo` function is updated, as per Listing 6-17, the tests will all pass once again.

Listing 6-17. Modifed `undo` Function to Resolve Failing Tests

```
...

undo: function () {
  this.set('complete', false);
}
...
```

While writing a test, it is often useful to use test data, to easily modify the state of your application while running tests. In the next section, we'll explore the use of Grunt to generate or modify test fixtures before running our tests.

Generating Fixtures

As shown in the last section, having a suite of tests that can be automatically run each time you make a change to your application can be powerful, and this is particularly useful for large, complex applications for which the time required to manually test is far greater than that for running a suite of automated tests. However, as the complexity grows within an application, it is likely that you will want to test the various states that an application can and cannot transition between. This is where a set of test fixtures can become helpful, as it allows you to quickly switch your application context, based on the data that is loaded into your application.

As the name suggests, fixtures are typically known and predefined. However, from time to time, you may require fixtures that are partially dynamic, for instance, if you want to verify that your application responds correctly to dates in the future. If you have a fixed date, you either have to ensure your application is configured to run within a given time period or modify your text fixtures to ensure that their dates are always in the future.

Let's extend our example from the previous section by adding a new function to our Todo module. This function will determine whether the date has passed on the to-do item, essentially allowing us to find all to-do items that have expired. Listing 6-18 contains the modified Todo module, with the additional function `hasExpired`.

Listing 6-18. Modified Todo Module with the Ability to Check If an Item Has Expired

```
module.exports = Backbone.Model.extend({
  defaults: {
    'title': '',
    'date': '19/02/2015',
    'complete': false
  },

  complete: function () {
    this.set('complete', true);
  },
```

```
  undo: function () {
    this.set('complete', false);
  },

  hasExpired: function () {
    return new Date(this.get('date')) < new Date();
  }
});
```

Next, we have to add a test to ensure that our new function is working as expected. Listing 6-19 has the modified test module with a test for the hasExpired function.

Listing 6-19. Test Module Containing Additional Test for Expiration Functionality

```
exports.todo = {
  setUp: function (done) {
    var Todo = require('../../app/js/models/todo');

    this.todo = new Todo({
      'title': 'Test Item',
      'date': '24/02/2014'
    });
    done();
  },
  ...
  item_has_expired: function (test) {
    this.todo.set('date', '2011-05-26T07:56:00.123Z');
    test.ok(this.todo.hasExpired());
    test.done();
  }
};
```

In the latest test, we update our todo instance with a new date that is set in the past and verify that when we call hasExpired on the instance, the value true is returned. This doesn't appear to be too problematic, as the test will always pass. Imagine a scenario in which we want to start handing multiple to-do items that form a to-do item list. On the set of to-do items, we want to be able to filter all the active items, items that have yet to expire. In such a test, we must ensure that we always have available some items that have not expired, and also, as there are multiple instances, we do not want to bloat our test module with lots of data. In such a scenario, it is best to create an external file containing our test data and load the data when the tests are run. This introduces a new problem, as our test file contains static data, and we have to ensure that the test data is dynamic.

Automating Fixtures at Runtime

Grunt can be used to automate the production of dynamic test data before each test run. To achieve this, we can use another Grunt plug-in called grunt-text-replace. Grunt-text-replace, as the name suggests, allows you to configure the plug-in to replace text patterns within a file and output the result to another location. To get started, let's first install the plug-in, as shown in Listing 6-20.

Listing 6-20. Installing grunt-text-replace

```
npm install -save-dev grunt-text-replace
```

Before configuring the task, let's generate our static test data and save it in the `build` folder. Inside the `build` folder of our application, let's create a new folder called `fixtures`. Inside the new `fixtures` folder, we can create our to-do fixtures in a file named `todo.json`. Listing 6-21 contains our test fixtures, with all items that require future dates having the value `FUTURE_DATE` as a placeholder. Now that we have our baseline text fixtures, we can start to configure grunt-text-replace to generate our fixtures that will be used each time we run our tests.

Listing 6-21. Testing Fixtures for Our To-Do Items

```
[
  {
    "title": "Past Item",
    "date": "2011-05-26T07:56:00.123Z"
  },
  {
    "title": "Future item 1",
    "date": "FUTURE_DATE"
  },
  {
    "title": "Future item 2",
    "date": "FUTURE_DATE"
  }
]
```

Listing 6-22 contains the task configuration for grunt-text-replace. The configuration for the target contains the source folders, the destination folder, and an array of replacements. The plug-in supports simple text swapping, regular expression swapping, or, as in our configuration, the use of functions to replace text within the source files. After the text has been replaced, the modified text is then output to the destination folder with the same name as the source file. In our example, files are read from `build/fixtures` and then written to `tests/fixtures`.

Listing 6-22. Configuring grunt-text-replace to Dynamically Generate Dates for Our Tests

```
replace: {
  fixtures: {
    src: ['build/fixtures/*.json'],
    dest: 'tests/fixtures/',
    replacements: [{
      from: 'FUTURE_DATE',
      to: function () {
        var today = new Date();
        return new Date(today.getFullYear() + 1, today.getMonth(), today.getDate())
      }
    }]
  }
}
```

Now that grunt-text-replace has been provided with configuration and a target, we can run it as we would any other grunt plug-in, using the grunt-cli npm package. Unfortunately, grunt-text-replace does not provide any feedback in terms of the files being read or written by default. To see which files have been written when running the task, you can use Grunt's verbose flag, as shown in Listing 6-23. Using the verbose flag will generate output similar to that featured in Figure 6-10.

```
jamescryer@Jamess-MacBook-Pro: ~/projects/progrunt-examples/c...

Running "replace" task

Running "replace:fixtures" (replace) task
Verifying property replace.fixtures exists in config...OK
Files: build/fixtures/todos.json -> tests/fixtures/
Reading build/fixtures/todos.json...OK
Processing source...OK
Writing tests/fixtures/todos.json...OK

Done, without errors.
james at ~/projects/progrunt-examples/chapter6/app
→
```

Figure 6-10. *Sample output of running grunt-text-replace with the verbose flag enabled*

Listing 6-23. Using the Verbose Flag to Output the Files Generated by grunt-text-replace

```
grunt replace -v
```

Applying Fixture Generation

Now that we have a set of dynamic fixtures, we can start to write a module that will handle our to-do list items. We will use a module of the Backbone library called Collection. Collections provide a convenient way of handling one or more models, tracking changes within a set of items, and applying functions to these too. Listing 6-24 contains the complete working example of a new to-do collection.

Listing 6-24. Backbone Collection to Handle Multiple To-Do Items

```
'use strict';

var _ = require('underscore');
var Todo = require('../models/todo');
var Backbone = require('backbone');

module.exports = Backbone.Collection.extend({

  model: Todo,

  activeItems: function () {
    return _.filter(this.models, function(item) { return !item.hasExpired(); });
  },
```

```
  expiredItems: function () {
    return _.filter(this.models, function(item) { return item.hasExpired(); });
  }
});
```

As shown in Listing 6-24, our collection expects to take a model that is an instance of our Todo module. The collection also has two functions for filtering the collection, the first to find all active items, and the second to find all expired items within the collection. To verify that our functions are working as expected, we can create a new test module in `tests/collections`. The file, as with our first tests, should be named the same as the module being tested but postfixed with `_test`.

Listing 6-25 contains the contents of `todos_test.js`, the tests for our collection. There are three tests for the collection: one to confirm the correct model is being used for the collection, another for verifying that we can filter the collection by active, and a final one for filtering the collection's expired items. An important section of the test module is to highlight the `setUp` function that is executed before each test. This is used to load our fixture data. Note that we load the `fixtures` file from within the `tests` folder and, hence, use the data generated from grunt-text-replace. This data is then loaded into the todos collection before being used within each test.

Listing 6-25. Test Module for Todos Collection

```
'use strict';

exports.todos = {
  setUp: function (done) {
    var data = require('../fixtures/todos');
    var Todos = require('../../app/js/collections/todos');

    this.todos = new Todos(data);
    done();
  },

  collection_has_model_of_todo: function (test) {
    var Todo = require('../../app/js/models/todo');
    test.equal(this.todos.model, Todo);
    test.done();
  },

  collection_can_filter_active_items: function (test) {
    test.equal(this.todos.activeItems().length, 2);
    test.done();
  },

  collection_can_filter_expired_items: function (test) {
    test.equal(this.todos.expiredItems().length, 1);
    test.done();
  }
};
```

Running the grunt-contrib-nodeunit task should generate the same output as shown in Figure 6-11.

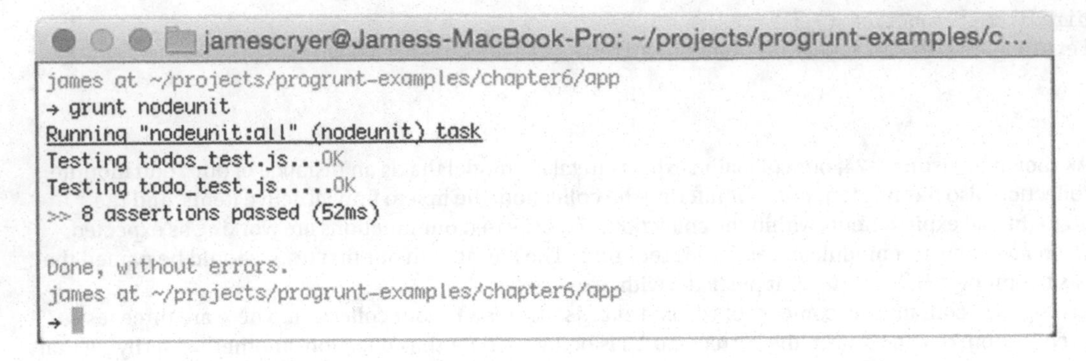

jamescryer@Jamess-MacBook-Pro: ~/projects/progrunt-examples/c...
james at ~/projects/progrunt-examples/chapter6/app
→ grunt nodeunit
Running "nodeunit:all" (nodeunit) task
Testing todos_test.js...OK
Testing todo_test.js.....OK
>> 8 assertions passed (52ms)
Done, without errors.
james at ~/projects/progrunt-examples/chapter6/app
→

Figure 6-11. *grunt-contrib-nodeunit with tests for both the collection and model being run*

Having a suite of tests combined with a set of solid fixtures that are dynamically modified through time can become invaluable, especially if you are working under tight deadlines, when mistakes can easily creep into a project. In addition to tests that work at a unit level, we can start to explore a higher level of testing. We can start to test our application in the browser itself—in fact, in multiple browsers. In the next section, I'll introduce a new Grunt plug-in that can help automate this process for us.

Testing in the Browser

The demands for more advanced and performant web applications have risen. As developers, we've responded by building highly interactive and complex applications in the browser. Pages typically have a larger amount of JavaScript running in them. The testing carried out so far has been exclusively run within the Node environment. In this section, we will look to write tests that can be run in the browser. This will ensure that our production code can run in the environment that closely matches the environment in which it will be run by our users. With the power of automation tools, we can run our tests in multiple browsers, which can help us verify the stability of our applications.

In this section, we'll explore using a new test runner called Karma. The team behind the popular front-end framework AngularJS developed Karma. The Karma project aims to make test-driven development easier and fast, while allowing developers to run tests in real browsers. Karma can be used to run tests in local development and in a continuous integration environment. Karma is not a testing framework, but a test runner, and, therefore, integrates easily with popular JavaScript test frameworks such as Jasmine, Mocha, and many others. At the time of writing, Karma has support for running tests in the following browsers: Chrome, Firefox, Safari, PhantomJS, Opera, IE, BrowseStack, and many others. The core team behind Karma has also developed a Grunt plug-in for easily integrating Karma with your build process. The plug-in is named grunt-karma.

Configuring Karma Test Runner

To get started, let's install the grunt plug-in and add it to our project. Listing 6-26 demonstrates how to install the new plug-in, and Listing 6-27 contains the configuration to be added to our Gruntfile.js.

Listing 6-26. Installing grunt-karma

```
npm install --save-dev  grunt-karma
```

Listing 6-27. Grunt Configuration for grunt-karma

```
karma: {
  all: {
    configFile: 'tests/karma.conf.js'
  }
}
```

The grunt-karma plug-in allows you to choose how to define your task configuration. It allows you to define a configuration file or specific configuration as Grunt options. In our configuration, in Listing 6-27, we've opted to use a configuration file. The configuration file can also be overridden by specifying options within a target. For example, you can define common configuration in the configuration file and override particular configuration when running your tests within a continuous integration environment. Listing 6-28 contains the configuration that will be kept within the `karma.conf.js` file.

Listing 6-28. Karma Configuration File

```
'use strict';

module.exports = function(config) {
  config.set({
    files: [
      'tests/main.js',
      {pattern: 'app/js/**/*.js', included: false},
      {pattern: 'tests/specs/**/*.js', included: false},
      {pattern: 'tests/fixtures/**/*.js', included: false}
    ],
    basePath: '../',
    frameworks: ['jasmine', 'requirejs'],
    reporters: ['progress'],

    runnerPort: 9000,
    singleRun: false,
    browsers: ['PhantomJS', 'Firefox'],
    logLevel: 'ERROR'
  });
};
```

The configuration file contains settings for which files to load into the browser and the base path to use to resolve the files. The next configuration specifies the test frameworks to be used and how to report the results of the tests. The last set of options configures Karma to run a local web server on port 9000, and to run the tests in the browsers PhantomJS and Firefox.

Before we can run our tests using Karma, we have to install additional npm packages that contain the plug-ins for Karma to integrate with our chosen browsers and test frameworks. Listing 6-29 contains all the packages will need to be installed before we can run Karma successfully.

Listing 6-29. Installing Additional Plug-ins to Support Our Karma Tests

```
npm install --save-dev karma-jasmine karma-requirejs karma-phantomjs-launcher
karma-firefox-launcher
```

If we try to run the grunt-karma task now, we should see a browser window launch and a page similar to the one shown in Figure 6-12 loaded. Next, we must add an additional file to configure our test runner to work with RequireJS, providing the ability to load our application and test modules as AMD modules. Listing 6-30 demonstrates the new file `test/main.js`. This file will be loaded first when Karma loads the page. It is responsible for configuring RequireJS to have the correct paths. Therefore, when a module requests another module it depends on, RequireJS knows the correct path to require.

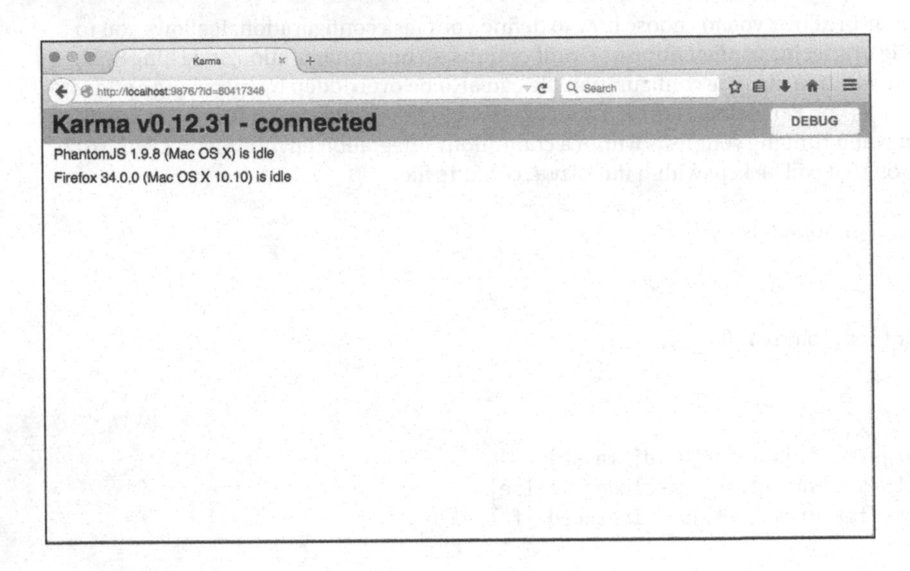

Figure 6-12. *Launching Karma in a browser*

Listing 6-30. Configuration to Support RequireJS and AMD Modules with Karma

```
var allTestFiles = [];
var TEST_REGEXP = /(spec|test)\.js$/i;

var pathToModule = function(path) {
  return path.replace(/^\/base\//, '').replace(/\.js$/, '');
};

Object.keys(window.__karma__.files).forEach(function(file) {
  if (TEST_REGEXP.test(file)) {
    // Normalize paths to RequireJS module names.
    allTestFiles.push(pathToModule(file));
  }
});

require.config({
  // Karma serves files under /base, which is the basePath from your config file
  baseUrl: '/base',
```

```
    // dynamically load all test files
    deps: allTestFiles,

    // we have to kickoff jasmine, as it is asynchronous
    callback: window.__karma__.start,

    paths: {
      'jquery': 'app/bower_components/jquery/dist/jquery',
      'backbone': 'app/bower_components/backbone/backbone',
      'underscore': 'app/bower_components/underscore/underscore',
      'fixtures': 'test/fixtures'
    }
});
```

Modifying Our Application to Use AMD

Now that we have the configuration in place to support running our tests, we should be able to start writing and running tests. Rerunning the grunt task and then clicking the Debug button at the top right-hand corner of the page should allow you to check whether your test files are loading as expected. Figure 6-13 illustrates a sample debug page that you will see at this point. Now that the test runner is loading correctly in the browser, you should notice a message in the console stating that no tests have been skipped. At this point, it is time to start adding tests to verify that our application is working as expected. We will revisit the tests written in the previous section for the Todo module. This time, the Todo module will be wrapped as an AMD module. The completed module is shown in Listing 6-31.

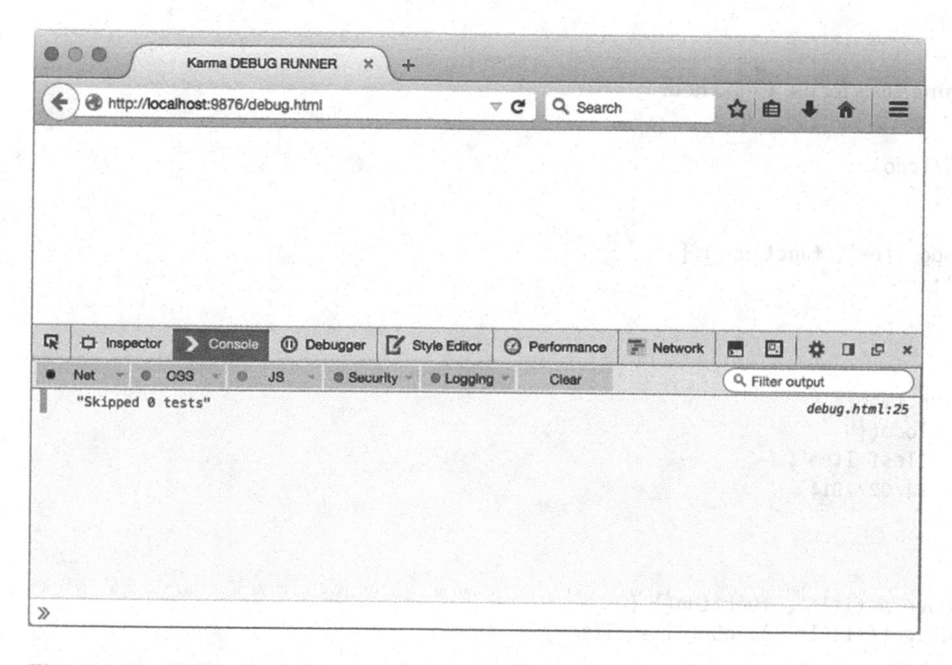

Figure 6-13. Debugging Karma tests in the browser

Listings 6-31 and 6-32 contain the to-do item and associated tests. These are of similar implementation, as shown in the previous section. These files differ only in that they are AMD modules and use the Jasmine test framework instead of nodeunit. Running the tests again will result in all three tests passing. Karma will output the test results to the console and also in the browser, if you have chosen to debug the tests in the browser. Figure 6-14 contains the output from grunt-karma in the console. You may have noticed that as you make changes to your application or test files, grunt-karma will automatically rerun the tests. Each time Karma runs, it runs the tests in all the browsers contained in the configuration and reports any errors within a given browser (see Figure 6-15).

Listing 6-31. Todo Module Wrapped As an AMD Module

```
define(['backbone'], function(Backbone) {
  'use strict';

  return Backbone.Model.extend({
    defaults: {
      'title': '',
      'date': '19/02/2015',
      'complete': false
    },

    complete: function () {
      this.set('complete', true);
    }
  });
});
```

Listing 6-32. Jasmine Tests for the To-Do Item

```
define([
  'app/js/models/todo'
], function(Todo) {

  describe('A todo item', function() {
    'use strict';

    var todo;

    beforeEach(function() {
      todo = new Todo({
        'title': 'Test Item',
        'date': '24/02/2014'
      });
    });

    it('should have a title', function() {
      expect(todo.get('title')).toBe('Test Item');
    });
```

```
    it('should not be complete', function() {
      expect(todo.get('complete')).toBe(false);
    });

    it('should be marked as completed', function() {
      todo.complete();
      expect(todo.get('complete')).toBe(true);
    });

  });
});
```

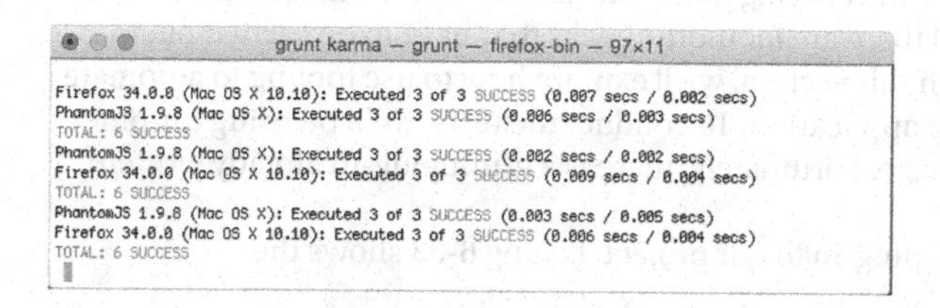

***Figure 6-14.** Output from grunt-karma in the console*

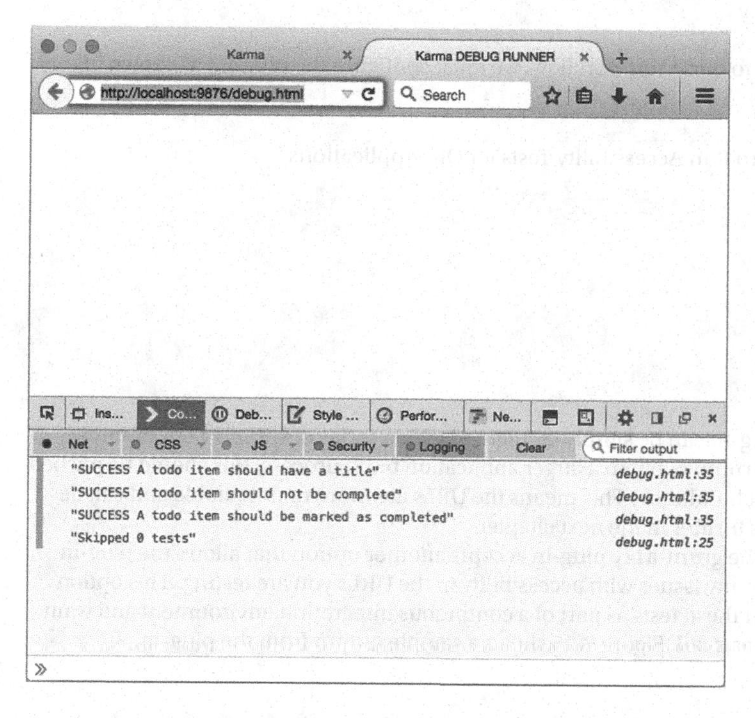

***Figure 6-15.** Console output in Karma debug view, containing the name of each test and its pass status*

In our example, we've only begun to explore the power that Karma can have in terms of testing your application. In a real-world application, Karma is capable of running hundreds of tests within each browser in under a second. You may also choose to run all your tests in all the major browsers employed by your users.

In the next chapter, we'll revisit grunt-karma when we set up a continuous integration environment for our project. We'll explore running our tests in multiple browsers in a virtualized environment.

Automating Accessibility Testing

Another key component of any test strategy for web applications should be accessibility testing. Accessibility testing should be conducted to ensure that everybody accessing your application or site has a positive experience and is not restricted from accessing your application features or site content. The mistake is often made that accessibility testing is only concerned with verifying that a site is accessible to those with little or no sight. Accessibility goes far beyond this, and there are far more checks that have to be carried out to ensure that a site or an application is accessible. In this section, we'll explore how to use tooling to automate early detection of accessibility issues within a web application. To conduct the tests, we'll be using Chrome Accessibility Tools to validate our application or page. Fortunately, there is a grunt plug-in already written that wraps the npm a11y package.

To get started, we need to add the grunt-a11y plug-in to our project. Listing 6-33 shows the installation process.

Listing 6-33. Installing grunt-a11y

```
npm install --save-dev grunt-a11y
```

Now that we have a11y available to our grunt workflow, we must configure the plug-in, as shown in Listing 6-34.

Listing 6-34. Configuring grunt-ally to Run Accessibility Tests for Our Applications

```
a11y: {
  live: {
    options: {
      urls: ['www.twitter.com']
    }
  }
}
```

As shown in Listing 6-34, the plug-in can be simply configured with a series of URLs. In our example, we've hard-coded the URL into our Gruntfile, but in a larger application build process, this should be pushed into a configuration file and loaded at build time. This means the URLs are more maintainable and can be shared across tasks. We'll explore this further in the next chapter.

In addition to the URLs option, the grunt-a11y plug-in accepts another option that allows the plug-in to throw an error, should it encounter any issues with accessibility in the URLs you are testing. This option becomes important if you want to run these tests as part of a continuous integration environment and want to fail your builds if the accessibility tests fail. Figure 6-16 shows a sample output from the plug-in.

```
jamescryer@Jamess-MacBook-Pro: ~/projects/progrunt-examples/chapter6/a...
Running "a11y:live" (a11y) task
a11y running

Report for www.google.com

  Text elements should have a reasonable contrast ratio

  #gb_119 > .gbts
  #gb_1 > .gbts
  #gb_2 > .gbts
  #gb_8 > .gbts
  #gb_78 > .gbts

  Meaningful images should not be used in element backgrounds

  #gbg > .gbtc > .gbt.gbtb > .gbts
  #gbi5
  CENTER > FORM > TABLE > TBODY > TR > TD:nth-of-type(2) > .ds:nth-of-type(2) > .lsbb > .lsb
  CENTER > FORM > TABLE > TBODY > TR > TD:nth-of-type(2) > .ds:nth-of-type(3) > .lsbb > .lsb


  ✔ARIA state and property values must be valid
  ✔Controls and media elements should have labels
  ✔These elements are focusable but either invisible or obscured by another element
  ✔The purpose of each link should be clear from the link text
  ✔The web page should have a title that describes topic or purpose


Done, without errors.
james at ~/projects/progrunt-examples/chapter6/app
→
```

Figure 6-16. *Sample output from running grunt-a11y*

The grunt-a11y plug-in reports issues with missing labels, ARIA properties, missing metadata, or low element contrast. This doesn't replace actual accessibility testing with another suite of tools. However, this plug-in can be used as an aid to help ensure that a baseline of accessibility is maintained within your application.

Exposing the Local Server to the Outside World

While developing your application locally, it is always convenient to be able to share and show your work-in-progress to others. Also, third-party tools sometimes need the ability to view your application on the open Web, to be able to work effectively. This is true of tools such as Google PageSpeed Insights or WebPagetest, which can be used to analyze the network performance of your application. Fortunately, there is a tool called ngrok that allows you to securely expose a local development onto the Web with a public URL. In this section, we'll explore configuring our Grunt workflow to allow us to easily expose our application.

ngrok is available as a binary download from `https://ngrok.com` and is also available as a Node module, which means we can easily integrate it into our Grunt workflow. To get started, let's include ngrok in our project, by installing the package using npm, as shown in Listing 6-35.

Listing 6-35. Installing ngrok

```
npm install ngrok --save-dev
```

To use ngrok within our Grunt workflow, we will register a task within our Gruntfile. Our new task, `ngrok`, is asynchronous, as it will send a request to the ngrok API to request a public URL for our application. We have configured our application to run on port 8000 locally during development, hence we pass the port number 8000 to the call to `ngrok`. The `ngrok` library returns either an error and/or a public URL. Once the URL has been returned, we can modify our configuration of other Grunt tasks to run against our public URL. For example, we can modify the URLs in our `grunt-a11y` task to run against a local development environment instead of a production environment. Listing 6-36 shows the complete custom task.

Listing 6-36. Custom Grunt Task for Running ngrok

```
var ngrok = require ('ngrok');

module.exports = function (grunt) {

  grunt.registerTask('ngrok', 'Running ngrok', function () {
    var done = this.async();
    var port = 8000;

    ngrok.connect(port, function (err, url) {
      if (err !== null) {
        grunt.fail.fatal(err);
        return done();
      }
      grunt.log.write(url);
      done();
    });
  });

  // Register default tasks
  grunt.registerTask('default', ['ngrok']);
};
```

If you are working within a corporate proxy, then it is likely you can combine ngrok with your other Grunt plug-ins to run these while behind the proxy. In the next section, we'll expose our application, so that we are able to run performance tests against our site.

Performance Testing

In this final section of this chapter, we'll explore the tools available to automate performance testing. We'll be focusing on network performance in particular, reviewing how optimized our applications are for delivery over the network. There are a number of great tools available for performing these sorts of tests. We'll be focusing on two plug-ins: grunt-pagespeed and grunt-perfbudget.

Grunt-pagespeed wraps the Node module, PSI. PSI is an abbreviation of *PageSpeed Insights*. PageSpeed Insights is a product from Google that allows developers to run performance tests either via a form in the browser, an API, or a browser plug-in. The Node module interacts directly with the API. The API accepts a number of parameters but primarily the URL of the site. The API then takes the URL, making a request to the API, and performs analysis on the requests generated from the page (e.g., requests for CSS). The analysis then applies a series of rules to determine the overall performance of the page, returning a single score between 0 and 100, where 100 is the most performant. The grunt-pagespeed module lets you define a threshold that must be achieved each time the performance test is run. If the threshold is not met, the plug-in will throw an error. This is particularly useful if you want to run performance testing as part of your build process, to verify the performance before releasing to production. The plug-in also supports a number of output formats, including TAP and JSON.

Grunt-perfbudget interacts with another performance tool similar to PageSpeed Insights known as WebPagetest. As with PageSpeed Insights, the WebPagetest can be used in a number of ways, via a web form, an API, or run on your own installation. The Grunt plug-in uses the public API; however, it can be configured to run against a local installation of WebPagetest. Grunt-perfbudget differs from grunt-pagespeed, as it allows you to define performance thresholds for each metric (e.g., the number of requests).

Let's get started by installing both plug-ins at the same time (see Listing 6-37).

Listing 6-37. Installing grunt-pagespeed and grunt-perfbudget

```
npm install grunt-pagespeed grunt-perfbudget --save-dev
```

Now that both plug-ins are available, we must configure each of them. We'll start with grunt-pagespeed, with the configuration shown in Listing 6-38.

Listing 6-38. grunt-pagespeed Configuration

```
pagespeed: {
  options: {
    nokey: true,
    url: "https://developers.google.com"
  },
  prod: {
    options: {
      locale: "en_GB",
      strategy: "desktop",
      threshold: 80
    }
  }
}
```

Grunt-pagespeed allows you to define a number of parameters that will modify the tests run against the URLs supplied. In our example, we're testing a single URL: `https://developers.google.com`; however, the plug-in has support for running tests against multiple URLs, with each being checked against the defined threshold. In addition to the URL option, there are options available for setting the expected strategy and API key. The strategy determines the analysis to be performed on the given URL. This can either be mobile or desktop. The API key is the key available via the Google APIs console. However, Google offers the ability to use PageSpeed Insights with no key, as per our configuration. This gives you limited usage of the API, and if you intend to use PageSpeed Insights in production or your formal build process, then I'd advise setting an API key. In our example, we've also set the threshold to a value of 80, meaning that if our overall performance score is below 80, an error will be thrown.

Figure 6-17 shows a sample output from running the Grunt plug-in with the preceding configuration. As you can see, the overall score, strategy, and URL are defined at the top of the output. In addition, a breakdown of each rule is given, with the associated value with the size of the static resources grouped by type.

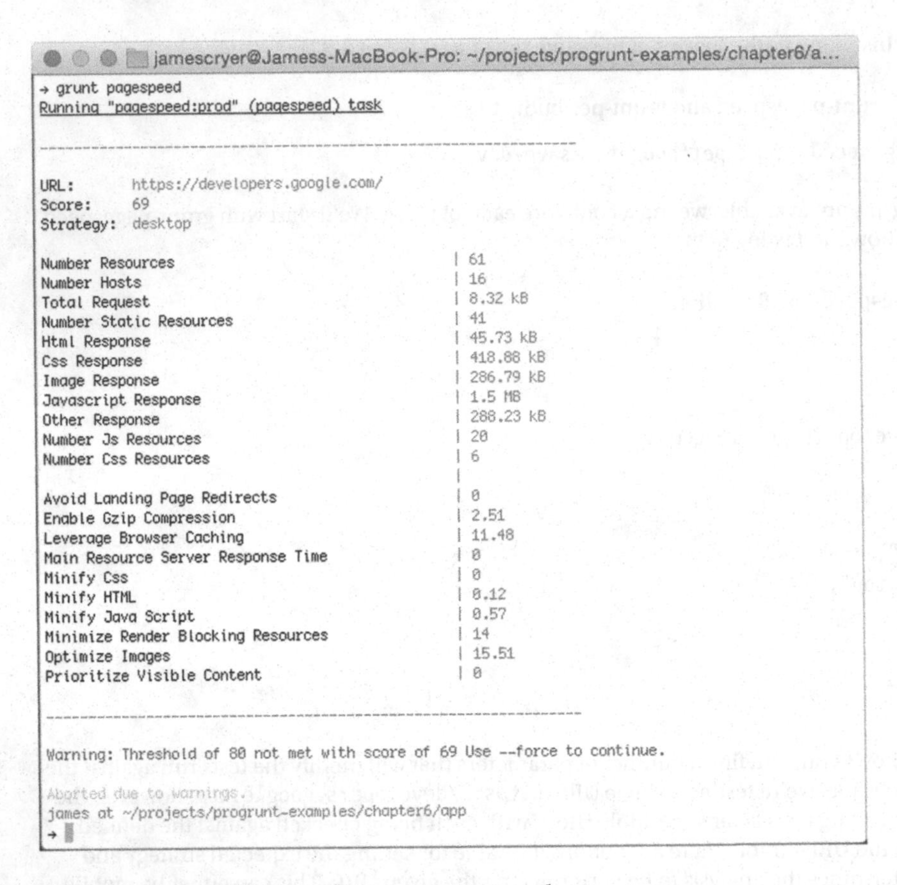

jamescryer@Jamess-MacBook-Pro: ~/projects/progrunt-examples/chapter6/a...
→ grunt pagespeed
Running "pagespeed:prod" (pagespeed) task
URL: https://developers.google.com/
Score: 69
Strategy: desktop
Number Resources | 61
Number Hosts | 16
Total Request | 8.32 kB
Number Static Resources | 41
Html Response | 45.73 kB
Css Response | 418.88 kB
Image Response | 286.79 kB
Javascript Response | 1.5 MB
Other Response | 288.23 kB
Number Js Resources | 20
Number Css Resources | 6
Avoid Landing Page Redirects | 0
Enable Gzip Compression | 2.51
Leverage Browser Caching | 11.48
Main Resource Server Response Time | 0
Minify Css | 0
Minify HTML | 0.12
Minify Java Script | 0.57
Minimize Render Blocking Resources | 14
Optimize Images | 15.51
Prioritize Visible Content | 0
Warning: Threshold of 80 not met with score of 69 Use --force to continue.
Aborted due to warnings.
james at ~/projects/progrunt-examples/chapter6/app
→

Figure 6-17. *Sample output from grunt-pagespeed*

Performancing Development Environments

As you can see, this can be extremely useful when working on a project for a long time. It can help you track any performance issues as they arise and ensure that your application is meeting a benchmark on each release. This is particularly useful if you are working on a project with many developers with new front-end dependencies being added on each release. It is good to also note that grunt-pagespeed can be combined with ngrok to test your local development environment before releasing your application to a public URL. Listing 6-39 demonstrates how this can be achieved, by revisiting the ngrok task from the previous section.

Listing 6-39. A Custom Task to Use ngrok and grunt-pagespeed for Local Performance Testing

```
grunt.registerTask('ngrok', 'Running ngrok', function () {
  var done = this.async();
  var port = 8000;

  ngrok.connect(port, function (err, url) {
    if (err !== null) {
      grunt.fail.fatal(err);
      return done();
    }
```

```
      grunt.config.set('pagespeed.options.url', url);
      grunt.task.run('pagespeed');
      done();
    });
  });
```

The key modification is in the callback passed to the `connect` function. In the last few lines, we use the `grunt.config` API to set the value of the grunt-pagespeed URL before executing the pagespeed task. The pagespeed task will then run with the URL returned from the ngrok service.

Next, we will integrate grunt-perfbudget into the project. This slightly differs from grunt-pagespeed, as we can define thresholds against each metric in the response from WebPagetest. Listing 6-40 contains sample configuration to be used to test our application.

Listing 6-40. Configuration for grunt-perfbudget

```
perfbudget: {
  default: {
    options: {
      url: 'https://developers.google.com',
      key: 'API_KEY_HERE',
      budget: {
        visualComplete: '4000',
        SpeedIndex: '1500'
      }
    }
  }
}
```

Running the preceding configuration will output the URL tested, the score for the given budget selected, and whether the budget was met. Figure 6-18 has sample output from grunt-perfbudget. As with grunt-pagespeed, if a particular budget is not met, an error will be thrown.

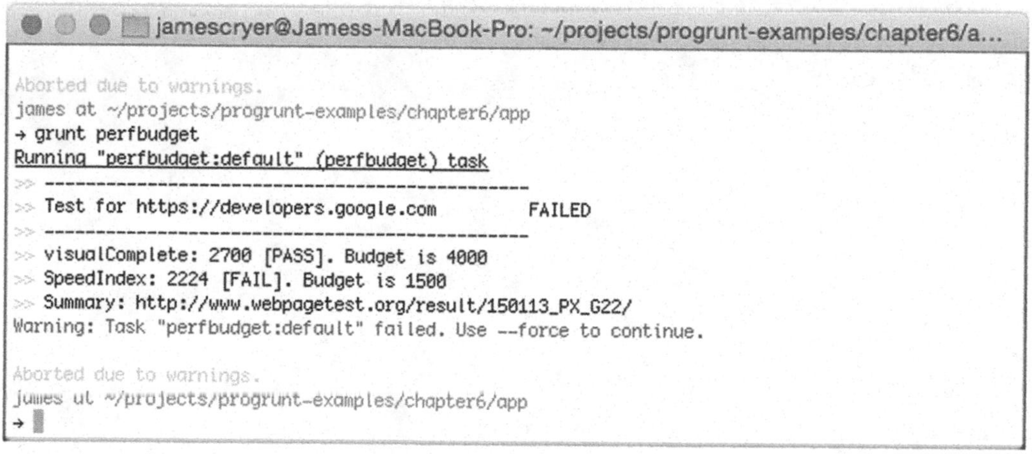

```
jamescryer@Jamess-MacBook-Pro: ~/projects/progrunt-examples/chapter6/a...

Aborted due to warnings.
james at ~/projects/progrunt-examples/chapter6/app
→ grunt perfbudget
Running "perfbudget:default" (perfbudget) task
>> -----------------------------------------------
>> Test for https://developers.google.com        FAILED
>> -----------------------------------------------
>> visualComplete: 2700 [PASS]. Budget is 4000
>> SpeedIndex: 2224 [FAIL]. Budget is 1500
>> Summary: http://www.webpagetest.org/result/150113_PX_G22/
Warning: Task "perfbudget:default" failed. Use --force to continue.

Aborted due to warnings.
james at ~/projects/progrunt-examples/chapter6/app
→
```

Figure 6-18. *Output from grunt-perfbudget*

As with grunt-pagespeed, grunt-perfbudget can be combined with ngrok to test local development environments, if you want to start to analyze page performance before releasing your application. To simplify testing large sets of URLs, both plug-ins can be used in combination with grunt-text-replace to dynamically generate a set of URLs. For example, if you want to test different environments, and the paths are identical in each environment, the domain or subdomain can be dynamically written while only having to keep a single list of URLs.

Summary

Throughout this chapter, we've explored how Grunt can be used to aid with setting up a local development environment, setting up test environments, and performing baseline tests against our applications in local development environments. We've explored the benefits of writing tests and how these can be run across a variety of browsers. We've concluded by introducing tools that can help verify that as we introduce changes into our applications, we do not introduce any performance bottlenecks simultaneously.

At this point, our Gruntfile has become bloated and unmanageable, with lots of duplication. Alongside our large Gruntfile, we're loading a lot of plug-ins each time Grunt runs, even if a single task is run. In the final chapter, we'll look at tools and techniques to make our Grunt workflow itself more optimized. The ultimate goal will be to have a lean and understandable build process that can be easily used by anyone within a team.

CHAPTER 7

Optimizing Your Grunt Workflow

In the previous chapters, we've concentrated on automating the build process to optimize our assets and ensure that they meet certain quality standards. In this chapter, we'll focus on optimizing your Grunt workflow itself. As projects grow, they typically become less maintainable, unless some attention is given to improve the maintainability. Your Grunt workflow is no different. As you start to use Grunt to perform more tasks within a project, you may start to feel that your Gruntfile is becoming a little unwieldy. Over the next few sections, I'll introduce techniques to ensure that as your project grows, your Grunt tasks remain understandable and fast.

Measuring Performance

As with all types of performance optimization, it is best to understand the problem and gather statistics to measure and analyze any changes made, to ensure the correct changes are made. In the case of Grunt, it is good to understand how long each task is taking to run and the overall performance of our build. This will ensure that we can reduce the time it takes to build our applications and also identify existing or new issues in the build. The performance of a build process is just as important as your application. In this case, we, as developers, are the users, but the same fundamental principles of usability apply. For instance, if our build process takes longer than one second, it is likely that our attention will switch to focus onto another task.

If you aim to introduce Grunt as your build tool to a team of developers, performance will be one of the concerns your team members may question you on. In this section, we'll introduce a mechanism to allow you to demonstrate the performance of your build and continue to monitor the build process as the project grows.

The plug-in time-grunt will allow us to measure the performance of our build. time-grunt displays the elapsed execution time of `grunt` tasks and differs from all plug-ins we've used so far. time-grunt does not introduce a new task; instead, it hooks onto the Grunt process to measure the elapsed execution time. Listing 7-1 demonstrates how to add time-grunt to the project.

Listing 7-1. Adding time-grunt to the Project

```
npm install time-grunt --save-dev
```

Now that the plug-in has been added to the project, we must update our Gruntfile to ensure that time-grunt hooks into our build process. Listing 7-2 demonstrates how to add time-grunt to our Gruntfile. In this case, we've added it to the top of our Gruntfile. The important part of Listing 7-2 is the passing of the Grunt object to the time-grunt plug-in, as this allows it to hook onto the `grunt.log` calls, to produce time measurements against our build. To measure the elapsed time, time-grunt uses another mpm module, known as hooker. The hooker module uses an approach known as monkey patching to modify the runtime of the original object being patched. With time-grunt, a pre-hook is used, so each call to `grunt.log` executes a function within the time-grunt plug-in, allowing it to measure the time difference between the start and end of a given task.

Listing 7-2. Adding time-grunt to Our Gruntfile

```
'use strict';

module.exports = function(grunt) {

  // Load time-grunt to measure performance
  require('time-grunt')(grunt);

};
```

With time-grunt now added to our Gruntfile, running our build should generate an output similar to the one shown in Figure 7-1. As Grunt completes the last task, time-grunt will output the time taken for each task to run, the percentage of time taken to run, and a visualization of the time spent on each task. The final output from time-grunt is the total time taken for all the tasks to complete. At present, our tasks take a total of 11 seconds to complete. Throughout the remainder of this chapter, we'll look at techniques to reduce the execution time of our build process and improve the maintainability of our Grunt workflow.

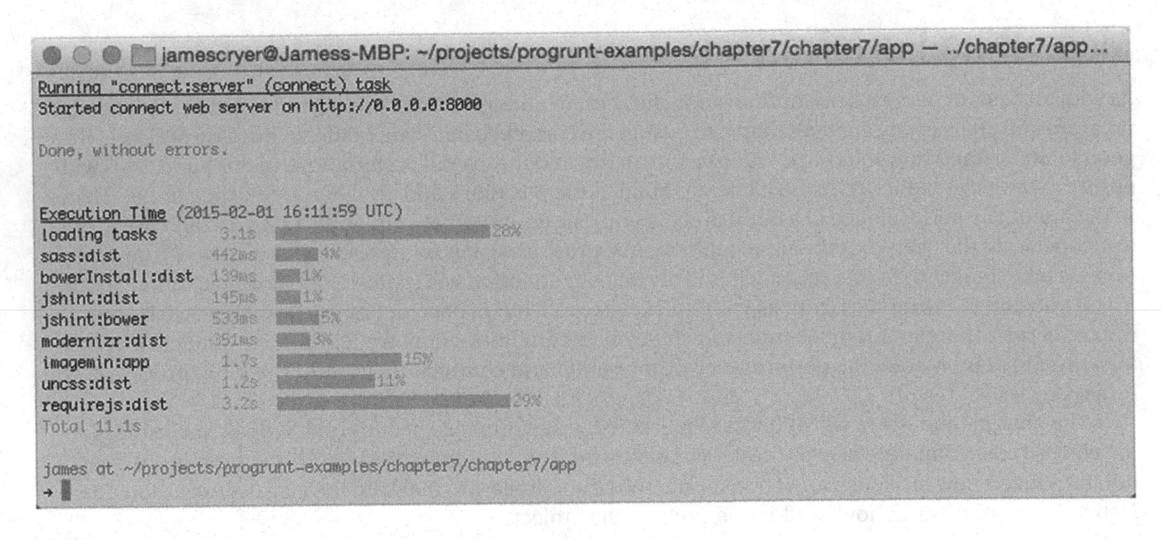

Figure 7-1. *Time-grunt output at the end of the last task*

Before starting a discussion on how to improve our approach on loading Grunt plug-ins, it is important to note that time-grunt will still output results, even if Grunt is stopped by a fatal error. Figure 7-2 shows a sample output in which grunt-contrib-jshint throws a fatal error, as an error is discovered in the application's JavaScript.

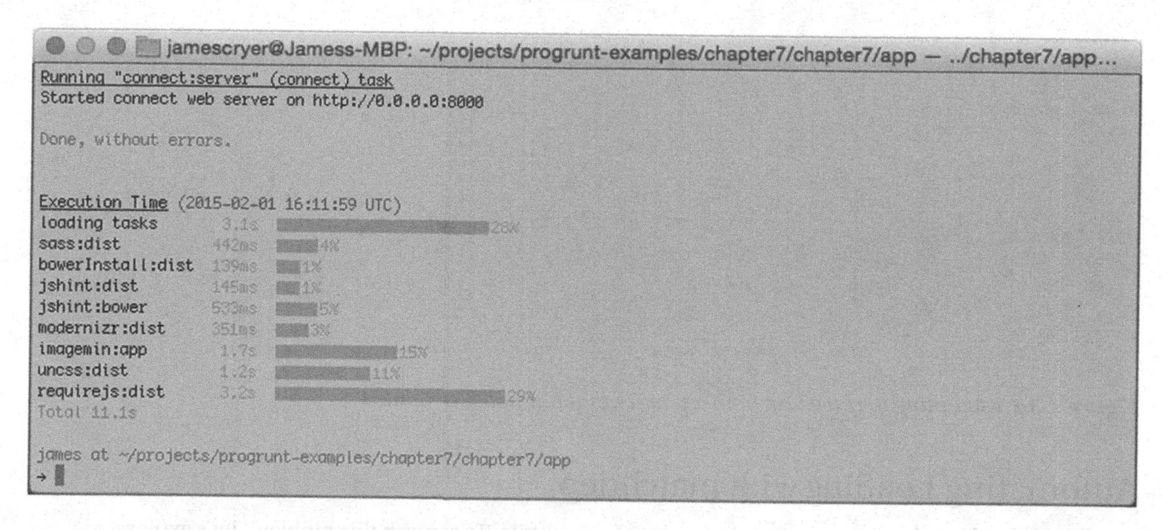

Figure 7-2. *time-grunt outputs even if Grunt does not execute all intended tasks*

Loading Plug-ins

In the first section of this chapter, we discovered that our total build time is currently taking a total of 11 seconds. The loading of plug-ins currently accounts for approximately 3 seconds of the total time each run takes for one of our tasks. In this section, we'll look at a few approaches for loading our tasks. Before modifying our Gruntfile to load plug-ins by an alternative method, let's revisit how we currently load plug-ins into our Grunt workflow. At present, we are loading plug-ins individually within our Gruntfile, as in Listing 7-3.

Listing 7-3. Loading Grunt Plug-ins Individually

```
grunt.loadNpmTasks('grunt-contrib-sass');
grunt.loadNpmTasks('grunt-bower-install');
grunt.loadNpmTasks('grunt-recess');
grunt.loadNpmTasks('grunt-autoprefixer');
grunt.loadNpmTasks('grunt-contrib-cssmin');
grunt.loadNpmTasks('grunt-contrib-concat');
grunt.loadNpmTasks('grunt-contrib-jshint');
grunt.loadNpmTasks('grunt-contrib-requirejs');
grunt.loadNpmTasks('grunt-contrib-handlebars');
grunt.loadNpmTasks('grunt-contrib-uglify');
grunt.loadNpmTasks('grunt-modernizr');
grunt.loadNpmTasks('grunt-bower-requirejs');
grunt.loadNpmTasks('grunt-uncss');
grunt.loadNpmTasks('grunt-contrib-copy');
grunt.loadNpmTasks('grunt-usemin');
```

The process of adding a plug-in each time we want to use it within our Gruntfile can quickly become costly and is error-prone. A common error people make is forgetting to place call `grunt.loadNpmTasks` after defining their configuration for a plug-in. Figure 7-3 shows an example in which grunt-modernizr is being run, but the plug-in hasn't been loaded in the Gruntfile.

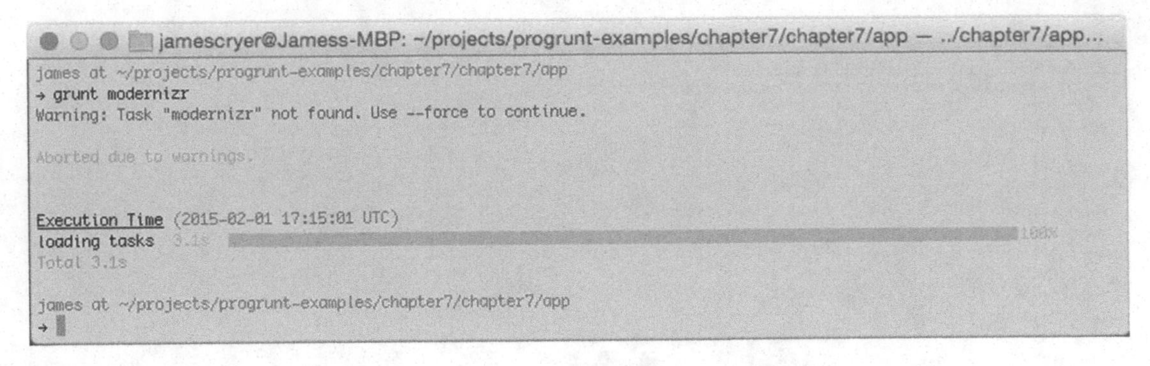

Figure 7-3. *Attempting to run a task from a plug-in that has not been loaded*

Automating Loading with matchdep

Loading individual plug-ins can take a large part of a Gruntfile. To remove this problem, let's explore automating the loading of tasks in our Gruntfile. The first module we'll use is matchdep, which has the ability to filter dependencies by name. matchdep will allow us to filter packages loaded from `package.json`, using a pattern that is supported by the minimatch library. If you remember, minimatch is also used by Grunt for its pattern matching on files. Therefore, if you feel comfortable with Grunt's file matching, using matchdep should also be easy to understand. Listing 7-4 adds the module to our project.

Listing 7-4. Adding node-matchdep to Our Project

```
npm install --save-dev matchdep
```

With the module now added to the project, we can now use it within our Gruntfile, as shown in Listing 7-5.

Listing 7-5. Loading Grunt Tasks with matchdep

```
'use strict';

module.exports = function(grunt) {

  // Load time-grunt to measure performance
  require('time-grunt')(grunt);

  // Load all grunt tasks
  require('matchdep').filterDev('grunt-*').forEach(grunt.loadNpmTasks);
};
```

There is a new line added to our Gruntfile in Listing 7-5 that is responsible for including the matchdep module into our Gruntfile and then using it to load our Grunt plug-ins. The matchdep module has a number of functions for filtering Node dependencies. In our example, we're using the `filterDev` function, which looks in the nearest `package.json` for the devDependencies and then applies a filter. Each function offered by matchdep returns the dependencies as an array of strings. In Listing 7-5, we take the array of dependencies and iterate each one and pass it to the `grunt.loadNpmTasks`. This final step ensures that all our Grunt plug-ins are loaded. We could target our plug-ins to specifically load all those produced by the core Grunt team. Listing 7-6 demonstrates the use of targeting a subset of Grunt plug-ins.

Listing 7-6. Loading Only Grunt Plug-ins Produced by the Core Grunt Team

```
// Load all grunt tasks
require('matchdep').filterDev('grunt-contrib-*').forEach(grunt.loadNpmTasks);
```

In addition to targeting dependencies by name, matchdep allows you to specify the location of the file containing your dependencies. Listing 7-7 offers an example that includes this feature.

Listing 7-7. Loading Dependencies from Another Location

```
// Load all grunt tasks from another json file
require('matchdep').filterAll('grunt-*', './build/tasks.json').forEach(grunt.loadNpmTasks);
```

In the preceding example, we've specified a location that the dependencies should be loaded from. Listing 7-8 contains the `tasks.json` used in Listing 7-7.

Listing 7-8. Sample Dependencies File: `tasks.json`

```
{
  "devDependencies": {
    "grunt": "^0.4.5",
    "grunt-a11y": "0.1.0",
    "grunt-autoprefixer": "^2.0.0",
    "grunt-bower-install": "^1.4.0",
    "grunt-bower-requirejs": "^0.11.0",
    "grunt-contrib-clean": "^0.5.0"
  }
}
```

Listing 7-8 contains a smaller subset of the project dependencies. If you now run grunt-contrib-clean, the task will still successfully run; however, if you try to run grunt-contrib-jshint, an error will be thrown, as the plug-in is not loaded. The ability to load different dependencies can be useful. For example, it provides the ability to load a different set of dependencies based on an option. Listing 7-9 demonstrates the use of such an option to switch the dependencies file used. Listing 7-9 loads an option called `deploy` that can be passed as a parameter to Grunt at runtime. If the option is set, then the file `./build/tasks.json` is used; otherwise, the `package.json` is loaded. This can reduce the time taken to load dependencies as part of a deployment while allowing the local development environment to run more complex sets of tasks. Listing 7-10 contains an example of how to pass an option to `grunt`. The option will return `true` if the option is set; otherwise, it returns `false`.

Listing 7-9. Modifying Dependencies at Load Time

```
module.exports = function(grunt) {

  var deploy  = grunt.option('deploy');
  var depFile = deploy ? './build/tasks.json' : './package.json';

  // Load time-grunt to measure performance
  require('time-grunt')(grunt);

  // Load dependencies
  require('matchdep').filterDev('grunt-*', depFile).forEach(grunt.loadNpmTasks);

};
```

Listing 7-10. Using Grunt Boolean Option, in This Case the Option Is deploy

```
grunt  clean --deploy
```

Grunt supports the ability for you to specify an option value, instead of using a Boolean option. For example, an option can be used to specify the environment. Listing 7-11 and Listing 7-12 contain examples of using an environment option to switch which dependencies file is loaded. This provides a flexible solution, as a new environment can be added quickly, simply by creating a new file then updating the environment option passed to Grunt. This could be useful if you had a different build for your development, continuous integration, and test and production environments.

Listing 7-11. Grunt Configuration Using an Option to Switch Which Dependency File Is Loaded

```
module.exports = function(grunt) {

  var env = grunt.option('environment') || 'dev';

  // Load time-grunt to measure performance
  require('time-grunt')(grunt);

  // Load dependencies
  require('matchdep').filterDev('grunt-*', './build/' + env + '.json').forEach
  (grunt.loadNpmTasks);

};
```

Listing 7-12. Using Grunt Option with Specify Value

```
grunt build --environment=test
```

Automating Loading with load-grunt-tasks

matchdep is not the only plug-in that can be used to automate the loading of Grunt plug-ins. Another popular plug-in for loading Grunt plug-ins is load-grunt-tasks. Both plug-ins are similar, but load-grunt-tasks has a more succinct method for loading Grunt plug-ins. Listing 7-13 demonstrates the most basic approach of loading Grunt plug-ins with load-grunt-tasks.

Listing 7-13. Loading Grunt Plug-ins with load-grunt-tasks

```
module.exports = function(grunt) {
  require('load-grunt-tasks')(grunt);
};
```

As shown in Listing 7-13, the amount of code needed to load Grunt plug-ins with load-grunt-tasks is less in comparison to the matchdep module. Load-grunt-tasks also supports the same powerful set of options that matchdep supports for more advance use. Listing 7-14 contains an example of using load-grunt-tasks to load dependencies based on an option passed to Grunt, which mirrors the same load process demonstrated in Listing 7-11, where matchdep was used.

Listing 7-14. Using Option to Modify Which Dependencies Are Loaded with load-grunt-tasks

```
module.exports = function(grunt) {

  var env = grunt.option('environment') || 'dev';

  // Load dependencies
  require('load-grunt-tasks')(grunt, {
    pattern: 'grunt-*',
    config: './build/' + env + '.json'
  });

};
```

load-grunt-tasks accepts three options: `pattern`, `config`, and `scope`. The `pattern` option allows us to filter by name which plug-ins are loaded, as we were able to do earlier with matchdep. The `config` pattern allows you to specify which json dependency file should be loaded. The `scope` option specifies in which type of dependencies you wish to search for plug-ins. The `scope` option allows the following values: `dependencies`, `devDependencies`, `peerDependencies`, and `bundledDependencies`.

Deferring Automating Loading

The ability to automate the loading tasks not only simplifies the addition of new plug-ins to our Gruntfile but also allows us to easily optimize our loading of plug-ins. We can now decide which plug-ins to load at a specific point in time. We can defer the loading of a particular plug-in until a task is run. Listing 7-15 contains an example in which we're not loading grunt-contrib-imagemin and grunt-spritesmith until our custom image task is run.

Listing 7-15. Defering Loading of Expensive Plug-ins Until They Are Used

```
module.exports = function(grunt) {

  var env = grunt.option('environment') || 'dev';

  require('load-grunt-tasks')(grunt, {
    pattern: ['grunt-*', '!grunt-contrib-imagemin', '!grunt-spritesmith'],
    config: './build/' + env + '.json'
  });

  grunt.registerTask('images', [], function () {
    require('load-grunt-tasks')(grunt, { config: './build/images.json' });
    grunt.task.run('imagemin', 'sprite');
  });

};
```

There are two fundamental changes in Listing 7-15. The first is a modified pattern passed to our first load-grunt-tasks call that excludes the grunt-contrib-imagemin and grunt-spritesmith plug-ins. The second change is the definition of a new task called `images`. Inside the body of our task, we use load-grunt-tasks to load our image dependencies, as defined in a separate file, before telling `grunt` to run the `imagemin` and `sprite` tasks. This approach will defer the loading of grunt-contrib-imagemin and grunt-spritesmith until we run the `images` task. Deferring the loading of a plug-in until it is needed will reduce the time taken to run all other tasks.

In this section, we've started to improve how we can load tasks by automating loading of plug-ins, switching loaded plug-ins based on options, and deferring the loading of plug-ins until they are needed. Figure 7-4 shows the output of our application after grunt-contrib-imagemin is removed from the main task. Our total time has dropped from 11 seconds to 9.1 seconds. The reduction in time isn't too significant but demonstrates how you can start to reduce your build time. Throughout the chapter, we'll continue to reduce time by adding further techniques to optimize the build process.

```
jamescryer@Jamess-MBP: ~/projects/progrunt-examples/chapter7/chapter7/app — ../chapter7/app...
Execution Time (2015-02-01 22:17:07 UTC)
loading tasks      2.6s   30%
sass:dist          452ms  5%
bowerInstall:dist  184ms  2%
jshint:dist        137ms  1%
jshint:bower       476ms  5%
modernizr:dist     352ms  4%
uncss:dist         1.2s   13%
requirejs:dist     3.3s   36%
Total 9.1s

james at ~/projects/progrunt-examples/chapter7/chapter7/app
→
```

Figure 7-4. *Reduction is overall runtime after our changes*

Organizing Your Gruntfile

In the previous section, we optimized how to load plug-ins into our Grunt workflow, and in doing so, we removed 30 lines from our Gruntfile. In this section, we'll be removing approximately 300 lines from our Gruntfile, as we explore ways of managing our task configuration in an improved approach. The previous section reduced the overtime taken for our Grunt tasks to run. The aim of this section is to make our task configuration more maintainable. The first step to improved maintenance is to extract our task configuration into more manageable modules. The second step is to extract all the hard-coded paths from our Grunt configuration into configuration objects, making it easier to share configuration across tasks.

Using Modules

To make our first improvement, we'll be moving our entire configuration out of the Gruntfile and into individual modules for each task. To achieve this, we'll be using part of the Grunt API to load our configuration in a single API call. Listing 7-16 contains our updated Gruntfile, which utilizes the Grunt API to simplify our Gruntfile, by using `grunt.task.loadTasks`. Using `grunt.task.loadTasks` will load all the files in the folder path provided. In our example, we specify the folder as `tasks`, and, therefore, Grunt will attempt to load files within a `tasks` folder relative to the Gruntfile. It is important to note that we are no longer making a call to `grunt.initConfig`.

Listing 7-16. Removing Task Configuration from Main Gruntfile

```
module.exports = function(grunt) {

  // Measure performance
  require('time-grunt')(grunt);

  // Load main tasks
  require('load-grunt-tasks')(grunt, {
    pattern: ['grunt-*', '!grunt-contrib-imagemin', '!grunt-spritesmith']
  });

  // Custom task for images
  grunt.registerTask('images', [], function () {
    require('load-grunt-tasks')(grunt, { config: './build/images.json' });
    grunt.task.run('imagemin', 'sprite');
  });

  // Load configuration
  grunt.task.loadTasks('tasks');
};
```

Listing 7-17 contains the contents of one of the files inside the `tasks` directory. In Listing 7-17, we use the Grunt object to add the config for each task individually, using the API call `grunt.config`. The interface for `grunt.initConfig` and `grunt.config` differs. `grunt.config`'s first parameter is the string of the property to be updated, while the second parameter is the value to associate with the property. In the new setup, the configuration for each task is stored in an individual file. This helps to maintain the configuration, as each module is focused on the task of configuring a single task. Splitting the responsibility of configuring our tasks over multiple files also improves the readability and makes it easier for new team members to clearly see where the configuration for each task lies. Previously, new team members would have to trawl through hundreds of lines of code to identify the part the configuration responsible for a given task. In the newly created modules, the configuration is typically fewer than 20 lines. Figure 7-5 is a screenshot of the files contained within the `tasks` folder.

Listing 7-17. Example Grunt Module from the `tasks` Folder

```
'use strict';

module.exports = function (grunt) {
  grunt.config(
    'jshint', {
    options: {
      jshintrc: true
    },
    dist: {
      src: ['Gruntfile.js', 'app/js/**/*.js']
    },
    bower: {
      src: ['app/bower_components/handlebars/handlebars.js']
    }
  });
};
```

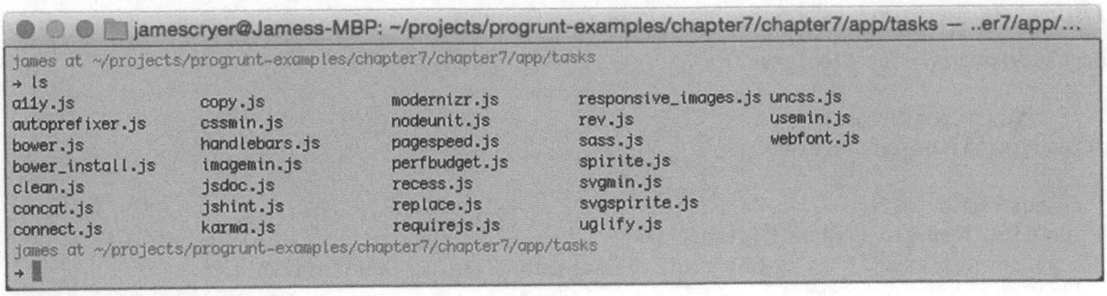

```
jamescryer@Jamess-MBP: ~/projects/progrunt-examples/chapter7/chapter7/app/tasks — ..er7/app/...
james at ~/projects/progrunt-examples/chapter7/chapter7/app/tasks
→ ls
a11y.js             copy.js          modernizr.js     responsive_images.js uncss.js
autoprefixer.js     cssmin.js        nodeunit.js      rev.js               usemin.js
bower.js            handlebars.js    pagespeed.js     sass.js              webfont.js
bower_install.js    imagemin.js      perfbudget.js    spirite.js
clean.js            jsdoc.js         recess.js        svgmin.js
concat.js           jshint.js        replace.js       svgspirite.js
connect.js          karma.js         requirejs.js     uglify.js
james at ~/projects/progrunt-examples/chapter7/chapter7/app/tasks
→
```

Figure 7-5. *All modules held within the* `tasks` *folder*

Using Groups

At present, we still have the definition of our default task within the main Gruntfile, and it is a large list of tasks. The next optimization to our Grunt workflow is to start grouping tasks into logical groups. This starts to add our own language to our task runner, which will help us communicate the ideas of our build to others on the team. In addition, it will allow us to target a specific set of tasks without running all the tasks. As we've moved the task configuration into separate modules, we'll create new modules within the `task` folder to hold our custom tasks. The new module created will be named `aliases.js`, as it will contain our aliases for other tasks. Listing 7-18 shows the contents of the newly created module.

Listing 7-18. Simplify Tasks by Grouping Them into Logical Groups

```
'use strict';

module.exports = function (grunt) {

  grunt.registerTask('prepare', ['clean', 'useminPrepare']);
  grunt.registerTask('css', ['sass', 'autoprefixer', 'uncss']);
  grunt.registerTask('dependencies', ['bowerInstall']);
  grunt.registerTask('js', ['jshint', 'handlebars']);
  grunt.registerTask('minify', ['copy', 'cssmin', 'concat', 'rev', 'requirejs', 'usemin']);
  grunt.registerTask('build', ['prepare', 'dependencies', 'css', 'js', 'minify']);

  grunt.registerTask('default', ['build', 'connect:server']);
  grunt.registerTask('serve', ['build', 'connect:dev']);

};
```

The module in Listing 7-18 defines a number of new tasks. Each task performs one or more other tasks. By grouping tasks together, we can start to build more flexible task runners for specific tasks. In our example, we have a generic build task that prepares the application for development and release. By defining a build task, we can easily load the application for testing or for development by simplify changing the last task that is run. Now that we have a basic set of steps to build our application, it is painless to add new tasks. For instance, let's add a test task, as shown in Listing 7-19.

Listing 7-19. Adding a New Task Is a Lot Easier with a Basic Number of Steps to Build an Application

```
grunt.register('test', [''build', 'karma']);
```

Extracting Common Configuration Options

The final optimization that we can make the organization of our Grunt configuration is to extract common configuration options from each task configuration. For example, instead of hard-coding the path to our `distribution` folder, we can define it once and reuse it throughout our configuration, following the principles of Don't Repeat Yourself. We can achieve this, as Grunt allows us to define variables within our task configuration. Listing 7-20 contains the modified configuration for grunt-contrib-cssmin.

Listing 7-20. Use of Variables in Grunt Plug-in Configuration

```
'use strict';

module.exports = function (grunt) {
  grunt.config(
    'cssmin', {
    dist: {
      options: {
        report: 'gzip'
      },
      files: {
        '<%= paths.css.dest %>main.css': '<%= paths.css.src %>main.css'
      }
    }
  });
};
```

By separating our task configuration from common paths such as the `source` and `destination` folders, we make our tasks less brittle and even increase the reuse across projects. To use this approach, we must define these variables in Grunt configuration. Listing 7-21 contains a new module that can be added to the `tasks` folder. This module will be called `config.js`.

Listing 7-21. Sample Configuration Module

```
'use strict';

module.exports = function (grunt) {
  grunt.config.merge({
    paths: {
      css: {
        src: 'app/css/',
        dest: 'dest/css/'
      }
    }
  });
};
```

The configuration module defines a set of key/value pairs that can then be used within our Grunt task configuration. Listing 7-21 shows a very small subset of the overall configuration required for the project. It can be extended to include properties such as the port numbers used for local development. As discussed in the previous section, we can also use grunt options to switch our configurations per environment, for example, if the paths differ on your local development environment compared to your continuous integration environment. Another good use case for having environment-based configuration is your test runner. Locally, you may choose to run only your tests in a headless browser, for speed and efficiency. However, in your test environment, you may want to run the tests against a number of browsers.

This brings us to the end of our discussion on Grunt configuration optimization. At the end of this process, our Gruntfile has been reduced down to 22 lines, and each task configuration is now managed by a separate module, with common paths being shared to allow us to easily update our project structure. Next, we'll return to exploring approaches to reduce the runtime of the Grunt task runner.

Running Tasks in Parallel

In the previous section, we started to group tasks into logical groups, which was a great approach to generalizing our task runner and communicating it throughout a team. Grouping tasks together has not reduced the total time; however, it does make our next optimization a little easier. In this section, we'll explore running tasks in parallel. As Grunt is a task runner based on files, the files output from a task are input into the next task, which leads to problems when trying to parallelize parts of the build. For example, we cannot run our CSS minification process until our SASS compilation has completed and output. However, there are sections of our build process that can be parallelized, for example, our CSS tasks can be run at the same time as our JavaScript tasks.

To achieve parallel running of tasks, we must introduce a new plug-in to the project. The plug-in required to parallelize our build is called grunt-concurrent. Listing 7-22 shows how to include the plug-in into the project.

Listing 7-22. Adding grunt-concurrent to the Project

```
npm install --save-dev grunt-concurrent
```

Now that the plug-in has been added to our project, we must define configuration. To do this, we create a new configuration file in the tasks folder (see Listing 7-23).

Listing 7-23. Configuration for grunt-concurrent

```
'use strict';

module.exports = function (grunt) {
  grunt.config(
    'concurrent', {
    assets: ['css', 'js']
  });
};
```

This configuration defined in Listing 7-23 is simple and defines a single set of concurrent tasks. The value assigned to the assets property is an array of tasks to be run concurrently. To run these tasks in parallel, you can use Grunt as with any other task. Concurrent tasks can be included in other tasks as well, allowing for a mixture of sequential and concurrent tasks. Listing 7-24 contains an updated version of our aliases module to use for the new concurrent task.

Listing 7-24. Using grunt-concurrent in the Aliases Module

```
module.exports = function (grunt) {

  grunt.registerTask('prepare', ['clean', 'useminPrepare']);
  grunt.registerTask('css', ['sass', 'autoprefixer', 'uncss']);
  grunt.registerTask('dependencies', ['bowerInstall']);
  grunt.registerTask('js', ['jshint', 'handlebars']);
  grunt.registerTask('minify', ['copy', 'cssmin', 'concat', 'requirejs', 'rev', 'usemin']);
  grunt.registerTask('build', ['prepare', 'dependencies', 'concurrent:assets', 'minify']);
  grunt.registerTask('default', ['build', 'connect:server']);
  grunt.registerTask('serve', ['build', 'connect:dev']);
  grunt.registerTask('test', ['build', 'karma']);
};
```

The build task has been updated in Listing 7-24 to now run our CSS and JavaScript tasks in parallel. Running our default task should allow us to measure whether there has been any performance increase. Figure 7-6 contains a sample output, and it may be surprising, but the overall time has increased—not the desired effect. To analyze the root cause of the problem, the verbose flag can be used to understand the performance decrease. In this scenario, the performance decrease can be attributed to grunt tasks being loaded a second time when grunt-concurrent is used. To resolve this issue, it is best to revisit the techniques used in the initial section and review which modules should be loaded as part of the main runner and the ones loaded for concurrent tasks.

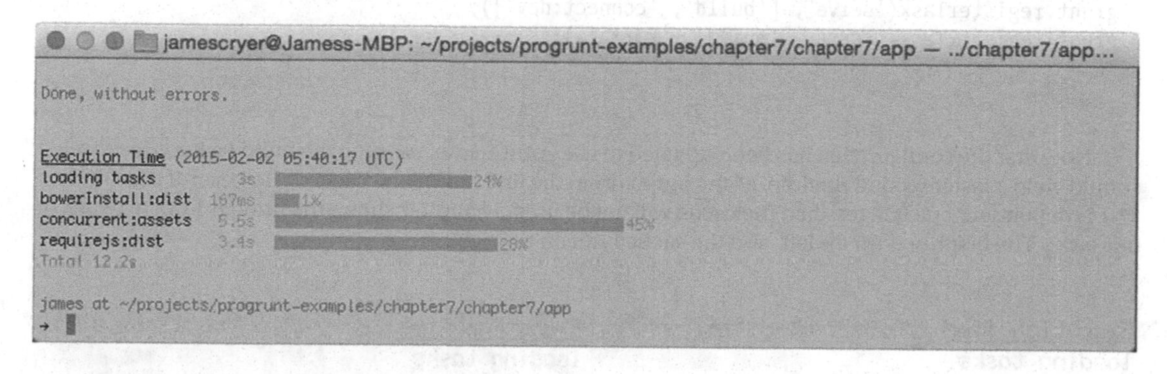

Figure 7-6. *Performance decrease introduced by using grunt-concurrent*

Running Things on Changes

In our attempts to optimize our Grunt workflow further, the next approach we'll explore is the use of a new plug-in known as grunt-newer. The grunt-newer plug-in aims to reduce the workload Grunt has to perform by executing a task only if the task's source files have changed. The plug-in itself does not require any additional configuration. Instead, to utilize its features, a task's name should be prefixed with `newer:`. Listing 7-25 demonstrates adding the plug-in to the project.

Listing 7-25. Adding grunt-newer to the Project

```
npm install --save-dev grunt-newer
```

To use the plug-in in our project, we have to update our alias module with the new prefix. Listing 7-26 has sample configuration to support this.

Listing 7-26. Modified Configuration to Use grunt-newer

```
'use strict';

module.exports = function (grunt) {

  grunt.registerTask('prepare', ['clean', 'useminPrepare']);
  grunt.registerTask('css', ['newer:sass', 'newer:autoprefixer', 'newer:uncss']);
  grunt.registerTask('dependencies', ['bowerInstall']);
  grunt.registerTask('js', ['newer:jshint', 'handlebars']);
  grunt.registerTask('minify', ['copy', 'cssmin', 'newer:concat', 'requirejs', 'rev',
  'usemin']);
  grunt.registerTask('build', ['prepare', 'dependencies', 'css', 'js', 'minify']);
  grunt.registerTask('build:concurrent', ['prepare', 'dependencies', 'concurrent:assets',
  'minify']);

  grunt.registerTask('default', ['build', 'connect:server']);
  grunt.registerTask('serve', ['build', 'connect:dev']);
  grunt.registerTask('test', ['build', 'karma']);

};
```

Now that the configuration has been updated to use grunt-newer, running the build task consecutively should yield a faster second runtime, as the output from the first run will be cached. However, if a file that a task is dependent on changes, then the cache will not be used. Figure 7-7 shows the timings from two runs of our tasks. The first run is on the left, and the cached run on the right.

```
Execution Time (2015-02-02 06:18:04 UTC)    Execution Time (2015-02-02 06:12:08 UTC)
loading tasks          1.8s                 loading tasks              1.8s
bowerInstall:dist    124ms  2%              useminPrepare:dist         23ms  1%
jshint:dist           69ms  1%              bowerInstall:dist         127ms  6%
jshint:bower         524ms  9%              handlebars:dist            30ms  1%
requirejs:dist         3.2s                 cssmin:dist                60ms  3%
Total 6s                                    Total 2.1s
```

Figure 7-7. *Measuring performance improvements from grunt-newer (cached run on the right)*

Reloading Changes Automatically in the Browser

Changes made throughout this chapter have improved the speed and maintenance of Grunt workflow. In this section, we'll look at another technique to improve the speed of feedback from our Grunt tasks. To achieve this, we'll combine grunt-contrib-watch with live-reload, to automatically reload assets in the browser. This will not reduce the overall performance of our Grunt tasks, but it will provide the perceived performance boost, as we will target which tasks are run, given the files that are changing. The plug-in grunt-contrib-watch can be used to watch a set of files and run a set of tasks when these files change. Listing 7-27 demonstrates how to add the plug-in to the project.

Listing 7-27. Adding grunt-contrib-watch to the Project

```
npm install --save-dev grunt-contrib-watch
```

Next, the configuration for the new plug-in must be added to the project. To do this, let's add a file to the `tasks` folder called `watch.js` (see Listing 7-28).

Listing 7-28. grunt-contrib-watch Configuration to Automatically Run

```
'use strict';

module.exports = function (grunt) {
  grunt.config(
    'watch', {
    css: {
      files: ['<%= paths.sass.src %>**/*.scss'],
      tasks: ['css'],
      options: {
        livereload: true
      }
    }
  });
};
```

Listing 7-28 has the configuration for the new plug-in. Each target for grunt-contrib-watch accepts two options: `files` and `tasks`. The `files` option is one or more patterns for files to watch. These are patterns supported by the minimatch library, as discussed earlier in the chapter. The next option is the `tasks` option. This specifies which tasks should be run when one of the files matching the patterns in the `files` option changes. In our example, we've added `livereload` and set its value to `true`. This final option is important, if we want to automatically reload our CSS in the browser each time we make a change. To integrate this fully in our application task runner, we have to modify the aliases module. The modified configuration is shown in Listing 7-29 by placing the `watch` task after the development server is launched. However, if you now run the tasks, the `watch` task will never run, as `connect` never exits. Therefore, Grunt will never run the new task. To resolve this, we have to make one last change by removing the `keepalive` option from our configuration. The `keepalive` option was originally used to ensure that the local development server was not shut down. As the new watch task does not exit, it continues instead to listen for changes in one of the files being watched and then triggers the associated jobs to run. Once the `keepalive` option is removed from grunt-contrib-connect, running the default task should generate output as shown in Figure 7-8. As shown in Figure 7-8, Grunt never exits unless it is forced to, as grunt-contrib-watch does not exit unless forced.

Listing 7-29. Updated Alias Module to Include grunt-contrib-watch After grunt-contrib-connect

```
'use strict';

module.exports = function (grunt) {

  grunt.registerTask('prepare', ['clean', 'useminPrepare']);
  grunt.registerTask('css', ['newer:sass', 'newer:autoprefixer', 'newer:uncss']);
  grunt.registerTask('dependencies', ['bowerInstall']);
  grunt.registerTask('js', ['newer:jshint', 'handlebars']);
  grunt.registerTask('minify', ['copy', 'cssmin', 'newer:concat', 'requirejs', 'rev',
  'usemin']);
  grunt.registerTask('build', ['prepare', 'dependencies', 'css', 'js', 'minify']);

  grunt.registerTask('default', ['build', 'connect:server', 'watch']);
  grunt.registerTask('serve', ['build', 'connect:dev']);
  grunt.registerTask('test', ['build', 'karma']);

};
```

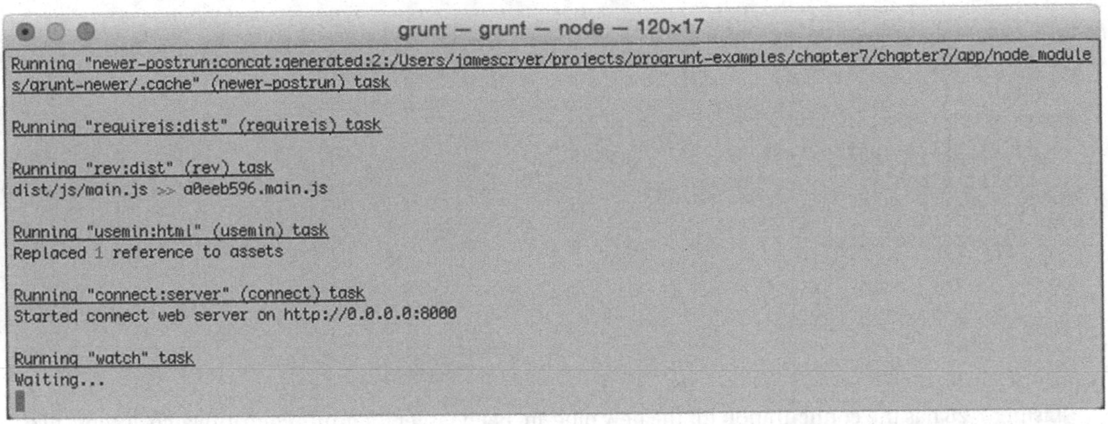

```
grunt — grunt — node — 120×17
Running "newer-postrun:concat:generated:2:/Users/jamescryer/projects/progrunt-examples/chapter7/chapter7/app/node_module
s/grunt-newer/.cache" (newer-postrun) task

Running "requirejs:dist" (requirejs) task

Running "rev:dist" (rev) task
dist/js/main.js >> a0eeb596.main.js

Running "usemin:html" (usemin) task
Replaced 1 reference to assets

Running "connect:server" (connect) task
Started connect web server on http://0.0.0.0:8000

Running "watch" task
Waiting...
```

Figure 7-8. *Default task running never exits, as grunt-contrib-watch listens for changes*

Editing one of the SASS files in our application will trigger the grunt-contrib-watch into action. This is shown in Figure 7-9. When the `main.scss` file is changed, the associated tasks are run. Next, we have to use the `livereload` feature of grunt-contrib-watch to automatically reload our CSS in the browser. By setting the `livereload` option to `true`, grunt-contrib-watch will launch a small HTTP server that emits events when files change to any clients listening for changes. The next step to get our setup working fully is to inject the JavaScript into our web page, to listen for changes emitted by the `livereload` server created by grunt-contrib-watch. To achieve this, we can use a livereload plug-in available for both Firefox and Chrome. The Chrome plug-in is available from the Chrome Web Store, and once installed, a simple click of a button will inject the JavaScript into the page. Figure 7-10 shows the button in a Chrome browser. It is important to note that the `livereload` server must be available before clicking the button to enable LiveReload.

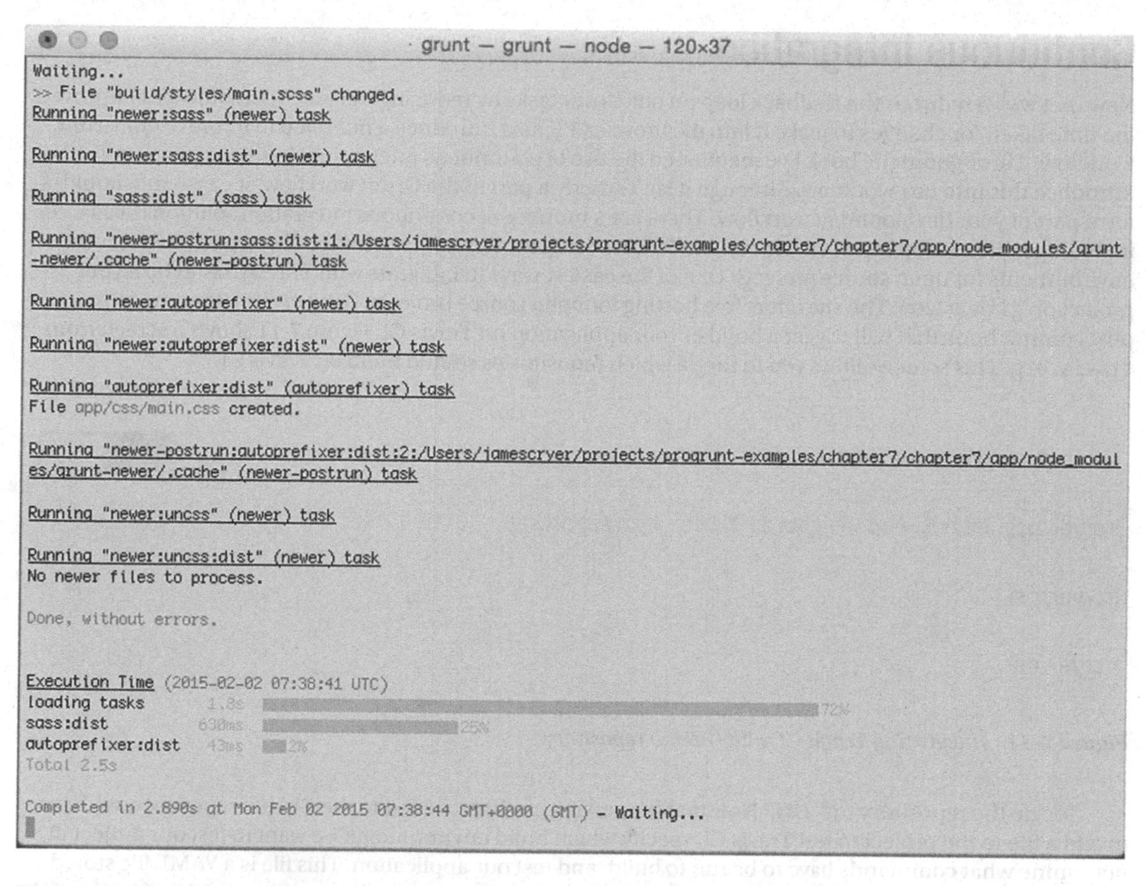

Figure 7-9. *Output as grunt-contrib-watch runs registered tasks, due to a file change*

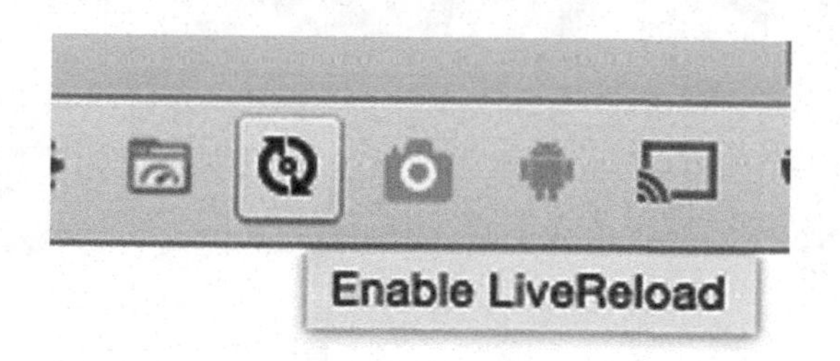

Figure 7-10. *LiveReload button for enabling LiveReload within our application*

The ability to automatically reload assets in the browser is powerful. It can reduce the need to leave your favorite text editor, as the browser will continue to refresh itself in the background, so that you can instantly see the outcome of your changes. As stated in the beginning of this section, grunt-contrib-watch does not reduce the execution time of our tasks, but it does speed up our workflow by automating loading of refreshed assets.

Continuous Integration

Now that we've reduced the feedback loop on our Grunt tasks by reducing the execution time and improved the time taken for changes to make it into the browser, I'll next introduce a final step to improve our Grunt workflow. Throughout the book I've mentioned the use of continuous integration. In this section, we'll introduce this into our workflow. Although it isn't strictly a part of the Grunt workflow, it can—andshould—form part of your development workflow. There are a number of continuous integration solutions available, including Jenkins, AppVeyor, and Travis. We'll be focusing on Travis CI, as it offers free open source build environments for open source projects. One of the easiest ways to integrate with Travis CI is to host your project on `github.com`. The site offers free hosting for open source projects. GitHub allows you to define a post commit hook that will trigger a build of your application on Travis CI. Figure 7-11 shows a screen from `travis.org`. This screen allows you to toggle which repositories should build on Travis CI.

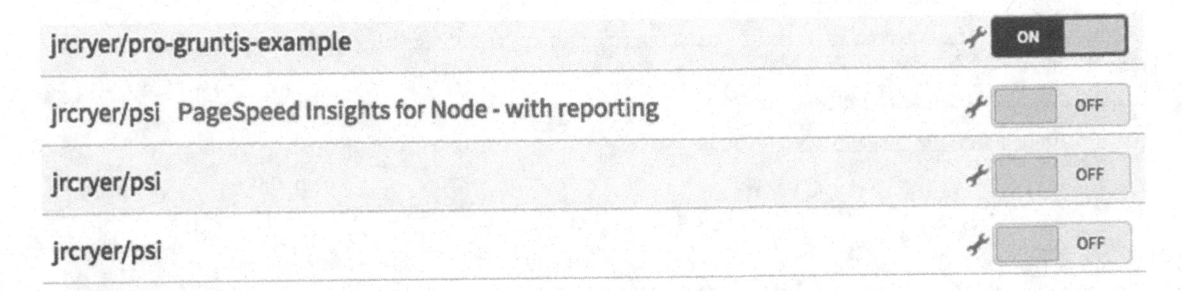

Figure 7-11. *Integrating Travis CI with GitHub repository*

Toggle the repository to ""ON." Now that the service has been added to the GitHub repository, we have to add a file to the project to test Travis CI, specify which build environments we want to test our project in, determine what commands have to be run to build, and test our application. This file is a YAML file stored within the root of the project and called `.travis.yml`. Listing 7-30 contains the contents of the `.travis.yml`.

Listing 7-30. `.travis.yml` Configuration for Travis CI

```
language: node_js
node_js:
  - "0.10"

addons:
  firefox: "17.0"

before_script:
  - npm install -g bower grunt-cli
  - bower install
  - export DISPLAY=:99.0
  - sh -e /etc/init.d/xvfb start
```

The `.travis.yml` configuration defines a number of properties for our project. First, the language of Node is defined, as we will be running our application within a Node environment. Next, we specify the version of Node we want to run. In this instance, we've chosen the latest stable version, 0.10. The next line defines an addon of the Firefox version 17.0 browser. We will be using Firefox to run our tests within the continuous integration environment. The next set of options defines a set of commands to run before our application is installed. The first line installs bower and grunt-cli Node modules that will be used to build our application. The next line is used to install front-end components for our applications. The third and fourth lines are used to configure a headless browser known as PhantomJS.

Now that we've completed the integration of Travis CI, every commit that is pushed to GitHub will trigger a build on Travis CI, and you will receive notification if the build fails. To ensure that tests run successfully, we have to ensure that our `package.json` file contains the correct test command. Listing 7-31 contains the modified `package.json`.

Listing 7-31. Adding Grunt Test to Our `package.json`

```
{
  "engines": {
    "node": ">= 0.10.0"
  },
  "devDependencies": {
    ...
  },
  "scripts": {
    "test": "grunt test"
  }
}
```

The importance of the `package.json` here is the `scripts` section of the file. Travis CI runs the test script when building the application. Therefore, it is important to run the correct Grunt task. With this final change, our project is now ready for building on Travis CI. Every time you make a change to the project, you will have the confidence of knowing that you are not breaking the project across multiple environments.

Summary

Throughout the book we've focused on optimizing our application developer workflow by continually adding Grunt tasks to solve common problems that we face in every web project. In this chapter, we took the opportunity to review our Grunt implementation, which had become bloated and unwieldy. We've introduced a number of techniques to reduce our Grunt execution time by seconds and improve the structure of task configuration, leaving our project in a state that is ready to adapt to our next set of challenges.

This brings our journey through Grunt to an end. I hope you've found the book helpful and that it has taught you new and interesting ways of using Grunt to improve your workflow. In an ever-demanding world in which the continuous release of new features in software is the norm, we have to help ourselves by using tools that automate and simplify tasks, to allow us to focus on the more difficult problems. Grunt is a powerful and flexible tool that can be used to automate any number of tasks, and if there isn't a plug-in available for your specific need, then a rich API provided by Grunt makes writing plug-ins simple.

Index

H

I

J, K

L

M

N, O

P, Q

R

S

T

U, V, W, X, Y, Z

Printed in the United States
By Bookmasters